"Clothes from a catalog, a dead flashlight.... Then, 'grief gives the ability' Kelley McKenna writes in 'A Free Pass.' From the poet's words ('Alone'), we read 'an attempt at order...'—and here our human nature almost collapses in a recognition of the 'other,' a co-struggle for sense, determination, amid disorder that nevertheless must compel us, as the planet does, just when 'a glimpse of a person who used to live in an ordered world' seems to pass by: the beloved. We are jolted by a past, present still. And we're listening. We who will have held loss in one hand and gains in the other...well, this is where we've all started: alone and not quite. The disappearance of things is tough stuff to say, so Kelley McKenna's poetry finds in each word sorts of finishings for shelter around which loss is terminal but temporary. Inside the poet lifts off the roof. Like Rilke's '[m]y hands are no longer mine' (his 'Flower Carrier'), this poet reaches for air and pulls back for herself fiber, 'naked through the rooms of my enormous house, rubbing the walls as if maybe he had disappeared into them,' a feeling we've each had, if we are honest about our grief and privacy. As Kelley McKenna's poems are well open enough to suggest, in dark days we will feel the hard facts of being alive. We may be amid the lovely, spontaneous, joys, and in our rising--like this poetry--from near collapse we can regain and imprint upon our imagination the surviving branch. As if the words are re-tracing, the poems make anew our experience: what we each watch, do, have loved. So, too, poems such as these rise out of love. Maybe beauty is a spiritual thing, even in the dark of caves, breathing warm air."

~   Peter Money
author of *Oh When The Saints*

Cobbled Bridges: A Multidimensional Travelogue

Prose Poems and Micro Essays

Kelley McKenna

illustrations and notes made by Jay Rossier
introduction by Iztok Osojnik

Cobbled Bridges: A Multidimensional Travelogue
© Kelley McKenna, 2022
ISBN 979-8-9850963-0-9

Introduction © Iztok Osojnik, 2021

Arson Press,
Brunswick, Maine, USA
https://arsonpress.wixsite.com/arson

Cover Design and Layout: John Reinhart

Cover images from Hubble Telescope, courtesy of NASA and "View of
London Bridge" by Claude de Jongh (1605-1663)

first, always, for Claire & Lily

and also for L & S

Introduction

This book of prose poetry and shorts spans two sides of a river with the reader positioned on the bridge, a place that exists as an in-between. Here we find a text that straddles literary genres. Through micro essays and prose poems, a narrative is formed, marked by a disjointed interiority. This is the state of chaos that is grief. Kelley McKenna finely carves small, precise images which reflect a ruptured sense of selfhood after loss.

The approach of death pulled husband and wife out of the routine of their lives and opened a world *between* life and death, where an unearthly love was shared, and a multidimensional hovering of the future cast its shadow. The narrator writes of the time just before, and following, the death of her husband. Though there is an experience of prolonged mourning, intense living radiates, as the narrator travels with a determination to "find" her lost beloved. The author does not hide behind sentimentality, nor does she curb the narrator's expression of rage against societal norms, and call for "recovery."

I compare this collection to the artistic iconography of *La Divina Commedia*, Dante's ode to love both earthly and divine. The author has also written about a kind of conversion in Dante's cave in Slovenia. She skillfully represents this experience by using language reflective of Robert Pinsky's translation of *The Inferno of Dante*. It resembles the moment of the Divine Comedy when Dante and Virgil "clamber down Satan's ragged fur, feet-first."

When they reach Satan's genitalia, the poets pass through the center of the universe, from the Northern Hemisphere of land to the Southern Hemisphere of water. Love and death, in their supreme experience, walk hand in hand.

The reader should not forget that the book is not a nonfiction description of a personal experience or a journalistic report, but a work of literature. The fragmented story opens a world both geographic and symbolic. It is a representation of an individual experience that goes beyond an account of a particular event or person. Its literary powers draw the reader into realms that are both real and other-worldly in the sense of magic realism of Latin American novels. It reads as the traversing of the first two parts of the Divine Comedy. The Inferno and the Purgatory. The purgatory is Iceland, Canada, Italy. It then somewhat reaches its peak in Slovenia, which was a place the narrator's husband spent part of his youth, and a land she visited to search for his footsteps. It is a land of poets and poetry, where people dedicate a holy day to their great poet, Prešeren. Inferno has turned into a harsh memory, into the purgatory of getting up on one's feet again.

The pieces in this text are in chronological order and there are ten years between section I and the final section X. The narration before the husband dies is in the past tense and everything else is in the present, as though everything that has come with his death, comes urgently, and is upon the narrator at all times. There is no distance, no escape. But the fact that she has placed his life in the past-tense shows us that she is accepting, even as she rails against this reality.

In fact, raging against the truth of the physical world is a core component of the narrator's internal struggle. A story evolves, that of a human being who can see herself as she sees the world. This is the literary magic of her fractured narration.

From mention of *The Bridge on the Drina*, the last book her husband was reading, to the golden bridge in Norse mythology, and all the bridges in between, we can't help but sense that the narrator is, herself, the bridge: cobbled together despite tragedy, and full of an energy that enables crossing.

Iztok Osojnik
Ljubljana, Slovenia, 2021

Prose Poems and Shorts

PART ONE

"Out of a deep cut, opened in a biography,
a new being comes into the world."

~ Catherine Malabou

from *The Ontology of the Accident:
An Essay on Deconstructive Plasticity*

PART ONE

Ljubljana, 2015: Warm Sauerkraut

I stand in my Slovenian kitchen and contemplate a meal:
roasted potatoes and warm sauerkraut. I'm interested in the
bag of fermented turnips I got for one euro from a man who
scooped the handful out of a large wooden street-bin.

But I don't begin to assemble a meal.

I just stand here,

looking out the window at the red-shingled rooftops, and
mountain-peak castle and,

      as I continue to stand here,
      and continue to stand here,

      I feel my aloneness intensify
      and sounds of accordions become deafening, and
      shards of sunlight rage across the sky,
      through my apartment,
      blinding me, piercing my limbs and
      I flail about, grabbing
            at kitchen counters
            as dishes shatter
            and hard floors shift
            and the tip of the earth rises three stories,
tilting, grabbing my ankles, pulling me hard, pulling
me fast, until I am left in a heap on the cobbled
street near the river.

No one will want you now, but still, I stand up, watch

shattered wine glasses and bits of porcelain cups fall from my frame, wipe the dirt off my jeans, brush my hair, reapply mascara and eyeliner, touch my body, realize it's all here, no part of me left at home in Vermont, no part of me crumpled in the square, no part of me kicked into the narrow Ljubljanica river and washed away. I put on sunglasses, grab a helmet,

ring a bell,
pick up speed,
ride wild through the streets
of Ljubljana,

dodging everything.

I

Denmark, 2011

Humlebæk in May

Jay stood tall and professorial, composed, in the window of the Danish suite, his breathing so shallow, it was almost imperceptible.

He wore a mended wool sweater and plain-framed glasses, statements of practicality, Calvinist values on display, pragmatism worn with pride, anti-pretense of any kind. No false selves.

You're the most stunning when you first wake up, unadorned, and full of ideas, he'd told me many times when we sat drinking French-pressed coffee in bed, an indulgence I'd convinced him to share with me. Now we were having coffee three-thousand miles from home at a cancer clinic in Humlebæk, Denmark.

Sunlight poured into the suite which faced a cobblestone parking lot on one side and the Baltic Sea on the other. Sweden floating in the distance. A large sunflower painting hung over the queen-sized bed, made up simply with white linens and two twin duvets. An Ikea advertisement: wooden giraffe on the windowsill, glistening hardwood floors.

What are you looking at? I touched Jay's arm as he stood by the tight double-paned window.

Lena from Sweden is leaving, I think, he said. Lena from Sweden was one of Jay's fellow patients at the clinic. *I think that's her husband picking her up.*

We watched a stout man of about sixty, with a voluminous white mustache, get out of his car. His body was solid, robust, fully present on the earth, unlike my husband, who seemed to make no indent in the air around him, as though his thinness was fused with atmosphere. Then we saw tiny Lena from Sweden come out of the clinic, her belly swollen with ascites, *cancer fluid*, she'd told us at one of our daily lunches over the past week since we'd arrived. She'd been at the clinic for a month and said she couldn't bear being away from her village north of Stockholm, separated from Lars and their grown children. She'd talked about the old farmhouse they'd restored. Sometimes she spoke a sort of meditation out loud in broken English about how she blamed herself for the cancer, pancreatic, *the worst kind of all*, she'd said, citing the breathing in of the lead paint she'd chipped away at for years. *But we have a beautiful house now,* she'd said. *I just don't know why I came here. Time with my family is so limited. Lars wanted me to try everything, but nothing is working.*

It is! You look so much better than just a week ago, I'd said, unaware that my optimism was revolting, embarrassing, even cruel.

We didn't mean to be voyeuristic as we watched the intimacy of Lena and Lars' reunion in the parking lot. But Jay and I, each in our own way, were trying to penetrate a relationship transfigured by illness. We were desperate to understand our own alteration, indiscernible and raging at once.

We saw Lars look at Lena, his face becoming a deeper shade of red, swollen with tears. We saw them embrace long and tender. It was unbearable, and yet we held the gaze until Lena and Lars walked together into the clinic.

For a moment neither of us moved. Then I looked at my husband. His face was wet too. I noticed its sunken greyness for an instant, then retreated back into my hopeful, upbeat tone, exhausting and false. I couldn't bear to face the truth of Jay's illness. I couldn't call it what it was: terminal.

Alternative

He'd been diagnosed three years earlier with stage four prostate cancer. He was 47 and I was 39 when we heard the news on speaker phone in our cold Vermont house. We'd just built a fire in the woodstove, then sunk into each other, stunned. I made tea. Began a crusade.

I was determined to prove the doctors' prognosis wrong and relied on the skills and thinking I'd grown up exposed to from the world of the "self-empowerment" industry, where I heard capitalist gurus yelling to the crowds: *You can do anything! There's no such thing as a victim! We create our own reality!*

NO VICTIMS.

I was sure Jay could cure himself with positive thoughts, alternative healing techniques, and dietary choices. It didn't occur to me, except in occasional flashes where reality was undeniable even to the most delusional person, that he might actually not get well. That's why we'd come to the alternative cancer clinic midway between Copenhagen and Helsingnør. The doctor, Finn Andersson, was a steadfast advocate for doing whatever he could to cure each person's cancer.

Piece of cake for you to live a very long time, he'd say to patients.

The Danish doctor's bookshelves were full of Western medical journals and hundreds of books on things like

Chinese medicine, oxygen therapy, qi-building, massage and immunology.

But patients who came to the clinic often did so as a last resort, having gone the allopathic route and having been told, *no hope.* This would become true of patients who were there in spring on our first trip, and gone by our second trip in autumn: Tulja, an elderly woman from Norway, Hugo from the Faroe Islands, accompanied by five of his extended family members, Rachel, a forty- year-old mother of four from Ireland and two ladies from Sweden—Maria, who had good English and Teresa, who did not. All were sicker than anyone wanted to believe, but in a few months, those patients would be replaced by a new cast of characters lying in hyperthermia submerges and past-life regression sessions. The casts were interchangeable. They were all the same amount of sick. Only a person who could accept the truth that death was coming would be able to discern this.

That certainly was not me.

I have an orgone box session, Jay said with a sigh. *It's supposed to restore my 'qi.'* He suppressed an eye-roll.

How much of this trip was to appease me? What did he believe in and what did he not? I didn't wonder any of this at the time. I did not allow doubt. When I felt its approach, I bit my lip to ward it off. This was a mannerism I'd learned from my husband. He did it all the time. He bit his lip to hold back tears. Most often when he was overwhelmed by something beautiful.

Magical Thinking

I spent the bulk of every day sitting next to my husband and
imagining him well, believing in the power of my thoughts
as a "healing agent." I concentrated very hard on a version
of his body that was strong and mighty.

> But it's exhausting to lie.
> Even if you don't know you're lying.

So sometimes I needed to run, to escape, to delve into the
world of my own mind, a place where
not-as-much-at-stake-imaginings could

> soothe.

Simple fantasies. Like what it would feel like to wear a red
dress in black leather boots at the theatre, on a boat, in a
cafe.

*Would you mind if I take a bike ride instead of coming with
you to the session today?*

Good idea, he said and kissed the top of my head. *You need
to take care of you too.* Kiss. Touch. Merge. Touch. Kiss.
Merge. *I'm just going out for an hour.* Touch. *I love you.*

Danish philosopher, Søren Kierkegaard, whose presence
was everywhere in Denmark, called despair the *sickness
unto death.*

We fought despair with the delusion called *hope.*

Kalevala

We'd met through the children.
Not mine or his, but our shared students.

Jay had written a play based on the Finnish saga, *The
Kalevala,* for his tiny fourth-grade class in rural Vermont.
They'd been my own students for grades one to three and I
loved each one of them.

With ease, the children spoke the stories of seduction and
humiliation, unaccomplished feats and tragedy caused by
interacting with the Sampo, a talisman thought to bring
good fortune and healing. The cadence of Jay's textual
interpretation spun upward inside me.

The play was wonderful, I said to him when it was over.

Thank you for coming.

The character of Kullervo is so tragically sad.

Yes.

The tragedy of magic.

Yes.

I'd spoken to him once or twice before, but some mystical
warmth had me caught, tangled, inside the words of the
play. I wanted to fold myself inside the depth of his

language. It felt like longing—a kind of expansive sadness, immediate and urgent and strange. Instead I just said:

I brought some chocolate for the children.

That's so kind.

You have to open your palms, make a cradle. I unfolded my sweater, which held the candy, into his hands.

The big piece is for you.

He bit his lip.

The Clinic

Dramatic interpretations of Carl Nielson's piano
compositions and a somber lone cello playing Bach could
be heard at any time of day at the cancer clinic in Denmark.
Brightly colored portraits of people and landscapes and
flowers and peacocks lined the walls. In the middle of the
building was a long table. On it: thin slices of rye bread,
mounds of smoked salmon, herring, chunks of feta, green
olives, diced tomatoes, cucumbers in dill sauce, raw onions,
hard-boiled eggs, potatoes in cream, grilled eggplant,
capers, pickles, mushrooms, hummus.

*Mediterranean food for health and Danish food for
happiness. You need both to get well from cancer. And
coffee, of course, is a must,* said the doctor with a hearty
laugh. *It is a great joy in this life. To deny ourselves coffee
is to welcome death. So, good food, good coffee and most of
all: you must exercise every day.*

So as his energy allowed, Jay and I biked, stopping
sometimes at the Louisiana Art Museum, where we
wandered through sculpture gardens with ancient trees and
sweeping views of the Baltic Sea. Jean Arp, Max Ernst,
Henry Moore around each perfectly manicured corner.
Giant Calder mobiles moving in the wind.

We pedaled fast to the art store in Kvistgaard, bought paint
and paper with a plan to make fertile gardens and landed
suncliffs.

With rolled-up jackets around our waists, ready for spontaneous rain showers, we rode through wooded paths, over narrow bridges, following trails along the sea to Hamlet's castle, an airplane museum, an organic farm where we ate apples from large baskets and Jay talked to farmers about his *trinity approach* to the cultivation of land he did at home in Vermont: sheep, chickens, hay, a rotation, a circle of nature.

Movement felt like an awakening: the more Jay did, the more he *could* do.

We took the train to Kierkegaard's grave in Copenhagen, Isak Dinesen's house in Rungsted, a boat across the sea to Sweden, outdoor concerts. We consumed life, breathed it in, prismatic kisses on the rides at Tivoli. The Scandinavian sky of May, light until midnight, so clear, moon and sun over the Baltic Sea.

During this time, the whole world was inside my body, as though I was not separate from anything. *I am clouds, I am cake, I am coffee, I am kisses, I am me, I am you, I am, I am, I am.* I wanted to catch and hold Jay in my positivity, enshroud him in joy, in love, in the energy I had, the whole of myself.

I was always optimistic, a guardian of the hopeful. I protected our delusion, clung to it. No one could shake me. That's why I loved the Danish doctor. He was like me, sure that Jay would get better.

You must enjoy life to get rid of cancer, he said each day.

And every Friday night, music was handed out to patients, staff, neighbors. Twenty or more of us sat around a long wooden table in the middle of the clinic's living room. Coffee and cake with whipped cream was served. Someone played the piano and we all sang together in Danish.

Joyful singing makes cancer go away.

When we weren't at lectures on illness (presented in English because of Jay and me), at past-life regression therapies (I got one too), at hyperthermia water immersion, in the orgone box, at the local hospital for blood work, the experience was like a kind of weird vacation of sorts. But sometimes Jay got tired, his body in various levels of pain each day. Sometimes he told me to go out on the bike alone. Sometimes he couldn't eat the picnics I packed. I ignored these things. I let him rest. I ate what he could not.

Seeing

Some days in Denmark, Jay and I walked instead of biked.

We found a faded grey entryway with chipped paint, looked
through it, saw heart-shaped leaves on a tree preening in
the courtyard light.

We walked to the edge of the Baltic Sea, collected sticks,
watched scaffolding come down from a thatched house,

saw horseshoes over a blue gate.

We looked down a dark alley, watched a brick wall change
from red to brown when the sun shifted behind a cloud.

We felt the rain begin.

I saw Jay clutch his stomach and slipped my hand into his.
I wanted to give him my strength, my vitality. Could he feel
it coming out of my hand into his? I didn't know.

I saw a stack of stones suspended on a piece of twine
swaying in the wind at someone's door.

I saw myself suspended in the warm air, terrified to move.

Compelling Future

The adults of my childhood, devotees of self-help gurus,
believed that people could cure themselves of cancer with
positive beliefs and facing past traumas. They told us that
Jay must create a *compelling future* in order to give his
body the *message* that it needed to heal. For that future
great life. Okay, yes, good, let's work on that.

But talk of the future unnerved Jay. He could only be in the
moment, doing the hard work of managing pain and
symptoms of disease. So I invented scenarios for the both
of us, convinced that Jay's body could heal from my
thoughts of
                    a shared compelling future.

When we first met, we'd talked about having a baby
together. So I imagined the baby every day in Denmark.
Sometimes I walked through the graveyard next to the art
museum and looked at the Danish names: Brigette Helena
Mikkelsen, Nikolaj Henrik Christensen, Hella Thora
Henriksen. *Our baby will be Astrid if it's a girl and Johan if
it's a boy.* My thoughts about the baby became obsessive. I
believed that I was healing Jay by inventing, and
meditating on, a happy post-cancer life.

But of course, I was just desperate to turn away from the
truth of what my future actually held: death of the beloved.

Imagining the opposite was survival, a form of mitigation,
a method for obstructing crushing terror. I had to believe he
would get well and that the two of us would continue on in

love forever. Fantasy was how I survived. In my world, the glass was always half full. It had to be.

Sometimes during Jay's treatments of hyperthermia, where he was submerged in hot water for several hours, or other times when he took a nap in the afternoons, I read *The Cure of Poetry in an Age of Prose*, which sat on our bedside table. Jay was writing a collection of poems and reading whenever he could, though he'd grown tired of even that. I spent time with his books, so many poems came in the suitcase: Seamus Heaney, Elizabeth Bishop, Wallace Stevens.

I didn't know it then, but understanding poetry through the lens of Jay's mind, how he articulated life through images, would later become the center of my master's thesis at Dartmouth, and later still, the core of a Fulbright fellowship in creative writing and literature I would get. I was being formed in the margins of Jay's unforming.

Humlebæk in Autumn

Our second trip to Denmark was four months later. We were in a different room. It faced away from the sea. In autumn, the sky was dark most of the day. Jay didn't bike or walk. I'd pushed him in a wheelchair through the Boston airport, the Munich airport, Copenhagen.

I was still revoltingly optimistic. The doctors in the States said Jay was going to die. *Malicious assholes*, I thought, *unresourceful, stupid.* We needed Finn, our Danish doctor, a beacon, the promise of immortality. Our only hope.

The first night in Humlebæk, I used soap Jay had made from beef tallow the year before. I'd brought it to Denmark in a square-shaped plastic container. He couldn't reach his feet, stomach swollen with ascites, cancer fluid, so I sat on the floor and placed them in a bowl of warm water.

I like the smell of this soap, I said.

I put clove drops in it.

The warming spice. I held each foot in my hands.

It's like when Jesus washed the feet of his disciples, Jay said, tears in his eyes.

Only you're Jesus.

No, my love. He bit his lip to ward off more tears. *You're Jesus.*

I bit my own lip, put the bar of soap close to my face,
breathed in its warmth.

Warmth.
The opposite of separation.

Bleed

The change was gradual, and then, it seemed, all at once.

Jay stared flatly across the Baltic Sea to Sweden. My boot
dug into the wet dirt road. I held his hand with care. I used
my body to say *I love you, I love you, I love you, you're
safe, I love you, everything's all right, I love you.*

I wish I'd done that moment differently.

I'd dig my fingernails into his palm, make him bleed. I'd
twist his wrist 'til it fell off. I'd pick up jagged sticks from
the shore and slice him open. But he wouldn't even notice
the blood. So I'd force him to stop walking. *Look at me!* I'd
scream. *Look at what you're doing to me! Why did you lead
me so far into you when you were just going to leave me?*
He'd look at me for a split second. Then turn his gaze back
to the sea. He was already gone before he left. For months
and months and months. He couldn't see me.

It was the hardest thing of all.

Beeswax

Sometimes I rode my bike to the Steiner School in
Kvistgaard, bought colored beeswax for tiny sculptures,
then sat on the couch in the common room next to Jay
during his oxygen treatments. I made flower petals and
fairy dresses and houses with rounded edges. He made trees
with orange fruit. I left the unused pieces in a white bowl
from the kitchen and a white plate next to it for finished
things, where something new appeared each day: rainbow,
bluebird, butterfly, rose. Helle, another patient, made most
of the pieces. A forest conservationist from Southern
Finland, she talked to us about the trees in Lapland, how
they were out of her jurisdiction and had to be dealt with by
Greenpeace. I heard her talking. I heard Jay tell her he
wanted to visit Lapland and maybe do some work for
conservation. I looked away. Compelling futures
mocked me now. I could hear my own voice: *he won't see
the future.*

SHUT UP, I told myself. *You have to believe in his future.*

Sometimes I walked alone on the cliffs above the Baltic,
not noticing the mist turning to rain. I didn't open an
umbrella or put my hood up. Just stared across to Sweden,
drenched, shaking, as wakefulness slipped its hand, so
slyly, into mine.

I didn't know that in two weeks, after we'd gone back to
the States, Finn's clinic would be indicted by the Danish
National Board of Health and would be issued an
injunction. I didn't know that a month after my husband

died, seven months from the rain-drenched day on the cliff, Finn would be dead too. From stomach cancer. I didn't know that most of the other patients would also die. I didn't know. I didn't know. I didn't know.

II

Vermont, 2012

Lent

It was the season of Lent. We were aware of its austerity. It reflected our humanness. In every bite of food he could not eat, in every glass of wine I did not drink. I kept control of the house, the children, the schedules, the doctors, the pills, the two of us. I kept control of us. So that he could have order when there was none in his body. None in our understanding.

One More Summer Please

I just want to see one more summer.

Oh my darling, of course you will.

I pictured it:

> We'll lower the canoe into the Connecticut River. You'll paddle and I'll sing. Later you and Leigh will catch trout, make a fire, cook it up. You'll do the ice cream run after dinner with Silas and Claire, still light at 9. We'll eat vanilla out of white bowls. Lily will gather lightening bugs in a jar, then set them free. You'll read *Huckleberry Finn* out loud. The children will fall asleep and the two of us will be close to each other in the warm air, kisses caught and gently held, stars bright.
>
> *Look*, you'll whisper. *The moon is so full.*

Close in the Chickens

I sat at the hospital in New Hampshire, waiting while Jay had an evening MRI.

The alarm on his phone went off and flashed:

Close in Chickens.

Shit. The sun was setting. My mind went to fox, fisher, cayoot, owl. I glanced at the only other person in the waiting room, a large man in a flannel shirt.

My husband's alarm says it's time to close the chickens in. I hope they're okay.

No one's home to close them in?

No.

Where do you live?

Sharon.

Wild country. Lots of things to get your chickens up there.

I know.

I used to fish in that area. Not since the hurricane. There's some nasty stuff in that water now, propane tanks and the like. Blah and blah, I couldn't hear him anymore, and blah and blah. It was too much.

Stop talking to me. I shouldn't have opened the door. I didn't have the energy to stay with the conversation. *And this warm winter didn't freeze it all away. Didn't create ice and the kind of wash out we needed. Mud and ice and pollutants in the White River. Hurricane Sandy.....*

I couldn't listen. I was thinking of summer, the canoe, *the way you never wear shoes or socks. I'm thinking about the shape of your mouth, your teeth. I'm thinking of your hands. I'm thinking of the way you call me baby.*

I heard the man's tone change. It was one of regret. *This whole hospital is built on a hill and that's why it's so hard to walk from one end to the other. Going from radiation to oncology expends more energy than it's worth, especially when you're pushing a wheelchair. This land used to be one big farm owned by a fellow who had cows. Every night at dusk, the farmer would call them in and when they were all safe in the barn, the farmer would ring a bell that signaled it was clear to hunt on the land.*

I nodded blankly.

Summer, smile, ice cream, summer, smile, teeth, summer, smile, cuddle, hands, baby, baby, baby.

In the House

I was afraid to leave the house, the room. Afraid he'd die without me. I called the nurse. She told me I didn't need to worry about him dying when I walked away from the bedroom.

Typically what happens with advanced cancer is that the patient begins to sleep more and more. He will stop eating and drinking and this process will happen over a long period of time. It's not usually something that happens overnight.

But he's already sleeping a lot, I said.

And when he wasn't sleeping, he had that far-away look in his eye.

You there, I wanted to yell. *Where do you go with your music on your I- pod?! Where are you?!*

On his laptop, he pulled up a photograph of a bridge in Bosnia and stared at it for hours.

Where are you?

The Clothes I Wear

I wore the same clothes every day. They lacked a life beyond our white house on Broad Brook Road, beyond the halls of hardwood floors and walls of windows overlooking a valley of snow-covered evergreen trees and, in the distance, sheep pastures, the house where I opened a red door with a brass knocker and took packages of morphine from Federal Express men in crisp white shirts. All winter. All spring.

Since they said the cancer had spread to his brain, since he'd started slurring his speech and forgetting what day it was, since he'd become unable to walk without my help to the bathroom, since they told me he would feel no pain, would die in his sleep, since all of this, I'd started, in the secret places inside myself, to imagine what life without Jay would be. It was how I coped: imaging the worst outcome and rolling it around in my mind, envisioning possible ways I could live without him. But, of course, I was terrified of those thoughts. If I imagined my husband well, he would get well, and if I imagined myself in the future without him, he would surely die. Such was the power I thought my mind had. Such was the cruelty of the positivity movement I'd grown up in.

I was exhausted by the control I tried to keep. *We will beat this cancer. We will manifest a new reality. Jay will grow healthy and strong. He will become a survivor. I will act as if he is already a survivor, and he, in turn, will become one. There are no victims.*

I managed to look in the mirror, then quickly look back to my clothes. *If he leaves,* I thought, *I'll have to get rid of every piece of clothing he's touched.* It was not an intellectual thought. It was not a plan. It was just what I knew would happen if-

STOP IMAGINING A FUTURE WITHOUT HIM.

The scene played on in my head even when I tried to make it stop. The clothes. I was obsessed with the clothes.

Sometimes, when he was asleep, I sat up in the bed beside him, flashlight in hand, and circled things from a catalog. Dresses and tops I'd buy when I was no longer standing, tired eyes, looking into the bathroom mirror while he slept restless—calmed by morphine, fast-acting, and again restless, calmed by morphine, slow-acting. I circled two short dresses, three cotton and two wool cardigans, one pair of red tights. When the flashlight died, I moved to the ceramic-tiles of the bathroom floor: six camisoles. Pomegranate, asparagus, wildflower blue. Sierra, sunflower, saffron gold.

Don't imagine yourself in the strappy blue sandals and floral print overalls you see in the clothing catalog! That's something you'll only wear if you get rid of all your clothes. And you'll only get rid of all your clothes if your husband dies.

DON'T MANIFEST THE WRONG OUTCOME. KEEP YOUR MIND FOCUSED ON HIS FULL RECOVERY.

I was involved with the catalog. I had to be. When I looked at it, nothing else existed. It consumed me. Mornings I woke early and sat with coffee in bed, reaching for it, midnight markings scrawled, sizes written in, crossed out and rewritten, colors circled, notes to self, *wear on a hot day, at a café, for a day by the sea, with oysters and beer, on the plane.* A future drawn in the margins of the clothing catalog. I ripped the pages out and set them side by side, as though there was a movement forward. As if the dress I would wear on the plane, placed before the dress at the café, made the café far away. As if I would sit in a café far away. As if the day I would go to the café was part of a group of days that belonged to the world outside my white house on Broad Brook Road.

I looked in the mirror, but couldn't bear the contortion: impending heartache.

STOP.

I will manifest a new reality when the men's clothing catalog comes. I will circle things for Jay to wear—a zippered wool vest, brown suede wingbacks, green pinwale cords, black linen thug cap. He will be so dapper, so present, so strong and we will go together to the far away café. Yes, we will go together.

Release

I sing Beatles songs into his ear.

The possibility for insanity exists.
But I don't lose my mind.

Instead, I feel something searing through my body and
radiating in the room. It consumes me. I will come to
denounce the spiritual, enraged to have been betrayed by
faith. I will come to curse the divine, stop believing, travel
to strange and unknown places in myself. But in this
moment, I know what's here. I name it. *God.* There's no
mistaking it. At least that's what I am thinking as it's
happening. Later, when reason settles me, I will not be so
sure. But *this-moment-me* and *future-new-me* will agree on
the intensity of it, the permeation of love.

I stay next to his body and watch the sky through our
windows until the light moves across the back of the house
and over the trees in the distance. It touches my hair, makes
me know the face of alteration. I turn inside out, close my
eyes and imprint myself with this moment, this adornment
of love, this bestowal of indestructible radiance that will be
forever mine.

I'll never let you go, I say out loud into the blackening sky.
In this never letting go, there will be freedom. I'll be bound
to the excruciating light that lives in the darkest places.

Alone

I see a soft woolen blanket, a baby rattle shaped like a lamb.
I see a woman's plainly painted lips, the curve of her
fullness hidden under loose linen clothing. I see a climbing
trellis of fake morning glories beside a mountain of neatly
folded sweaters:

orange, grey, black.

I see an attempt at order, a tangible pattern, things
controlled, things aligned. I see myself in a
pentagon-shaped mirror. White glass beads along the edges.
For one second, I catch a glimpse of a person who used to
live in an ordered world. My beliefs crisply folded on
shelves lined with silk:

God, love, forever.

I look away.

The lady in the shop says *you're young, you'll meet
someone else, but wait a while, take some time with
yourself first.*

Right. Time with myself. Time with my own thoughts, my
own memories. Memories of his skin.

The skin that used to touch my skin. Time to remember
how his skin turned cold in my arms.

Time to remember feeling his arms as they stiffened. The

48

arms that used to hold me. How they couldn't bend.

Dead arms don't bend. I never knew that.

Time to wander naked through the rooms of my enormous house, rubbing the walls as if maybe he's disappeared into them.

Time to flatten my body against the perfectly painted eggshell smoothness, pretend he's holding me still.

No.

 I don't need time with myself.

The Episcopalian Priest

A triad was formed. Because of this, I called the priest on his cell phone in the middle of the night and he came. We were linked by the presence of something we did not understand. We were, the three of us, connected by mysteries beyond our comprehension. Jay and him and me. He guided us, then married us,

then

what?

The priest and my mother and I stand over my husband's body. I see that the priest is young. Maybe even younger than I am. Or maybe the same age. I never noticed that before. We stand here, the three of us. My mother and the priest and me. She cries.

I sit in a church filled with more than 500 people. I ask the priest to write down the instructions for what I am supposed to do during the service. He says, *just keep your eyes on me. I will make sure you know.*

I sit in his office and ask, *why are there so many old people still alive and Jay is dead?* He says we do not know the mysteries of this world. That's when I see that what we had is different now. Because I can't live in the mystery without Jay.

I sit opposite the priest in his office. But he can't comfort me as he once did. With only two, it's broken.

Later About the Priest

It's hard to admit, but I want the priest to touch me. I want him to hold me. I imagine kissing. Maybe he presses up against me in his office, maybe lays me down on the couch where Jay and I discussed our wedding with him.

It's just a sensation I have in my body. Not even a fantasy.

I read about this in one of Rudolph Steiner's books on anthroposophy. He was a philosopher in the 1930's, a devotee of Goethe. Steiner said that the spirit of dead people live in, and enliven, the sex organs of the people they leave behind.

What?

I go to a conference close to my house in the mountains of New Hampshire and ask some stodgy old anthroposophists about that theory. They're appalled, then dismissive. Say they never read that. Then I pull out the big gun: a photograph of my children's father, a look-alike for Rudolph Steiner. The old anthroposophists gasp and say that my ex must be the philosopher reincarnated.

You have children with this man?

Then I got some respect. But still, no answers.

But back to the priest and his hands on my body. I decide not to meet with him anymore. Another loss.

Broad Brook Road

This is what death is: me driving alone in Vermont,

        most often on Broad Brook Road.

Jay loved the back roads of Tunbridge, Sharon, Chelsea, Corinth, Newbury, Thetford, the more raw, desolate and cold, the better. He saw the harsh climate, the weathered voices at the country store, gnarled by smoke and cold, invigorating, and I came to see beauty in a place I had once endured as godforsaken, barren.

In his F150, we moved slowly past backyard rope tows on makeshift ski hills, to the Hunger Mountain Co-op in Montpelier with especially green olives and sweet wine in small bottles, then Bear Pond books. I got lost in the travel section, planning trips we'd take together, while he curled up in Poetry, meditating on just

        one line of one poem.

Then on the way home, we stopped at the shop behind the tire place in Chelsea, bought chicken feed and wool socks for cheap.

Often we drove by a yellow farmhouse on our road.

Someday I'd like to live in that house, Jay said more than once.

We didn't know the owner at the time, but someday in the

future, I will. And later, I will live in the yellow farmhouse with him. And then I will live there alone.

And I will be swollen with ghosts on Broad Brook Road.

Taking An Art Class

We are given a project to do. Here are the parameters. Lines parallel. Lines perpendicular. Clear relationships. Mass, plane, line. No diagonals. I put the safety glasses on. Cut the wood. Use the joiner. Plane the wood. Glue the pieces. Clamp the wood. On every side: no give.

I drive home. Say his name out loud in the car like I always do. *Jay.* I just say it. This was his car. I put my distance glasses on. They make me feel that something has changed. That I am different than I was. I am a person who wears glasses now. I am altered. He never saw the me who wears glasses. The me who takes an art class.

I bring my clamped box into the house, put it on the kitchen table. Make dinner. We are girls together sometimes. We all have long hair: yellow, red, brown. We record our voices. Try to tell who is who. We laugh so hard, we fall over in our chairs.

I am forming a new life for us, measuring every moment to lead us to now. I take what I need for me, give what they need for them. The boys are gone, left when their dad did. I sketch out each piece of newness, create a diagram for us to follow. Relationships clear: Mom, Lily, Claire. It's just us now.

Diagonals.

The Fox

A fox is out there. I know because I hear the chickens
making unusual sounds. At first I ignore them. But when
the chickens scream a second time, I leap up.

I know.

I race outside onto the large Vermont deck. There it is, in
the field below the house. With my dark-feathered favorite
in its mouth. It's the chicken Jay spared when doing
research for a *Hobby Farms* article: "Butchering Meat
Birds."

You've slaughtered birds before. Why research?

I lost the feeling in my bones.

What about that one? I pointed to the dark-feathered one.

I couldn't kill that one. She has too much life in her.

I stand on the top of my hill throwing sticks at the fox,
screaming at it to bring the dark bird back.

PLEASE!

I yell as loud as I can. It stops.

She's our favorite one, I say to the fox. It stares at me. It
knows I have realized my limitations. It knows I don't have
a gun. Not in the basement. Or the garage. Or even locked

up in a fancy cabinet. There's nothing I can do. I'm defeated.

My father trained me to believe that the only limitations in life are the manifestations of our mind. But I've long surrendered to the oncologist's call, the tethered touch, the slow decline, the futility of hope. There's no magic bullet. There's nothing to do.

You fucking fox.

I collapse on the grass as it bounds away.

Picking Green Beans With Lily

like Jay and I used to do before we stopped putting
things together: basil, garlic, olive oil, pine nuts. My mother
asked *when are you going to start cooking again* so we
drove to the farm and picked green beans, Lily and I,
Tunbridge Hill, Vermont, where we all went contra dancing
two summers ago, spinning barefoot in the barn, skirt
twirling out laughter, the children watching love on a
sawdust dance floor. Who am I now picking green beans
with Lily? The wind blowing, the scent of tarragon.

Four Aces

I meet a man with green hair at a diner in White River
Junction and he tells me things I don't want to hear. About
the blur years when I rejected everyone in my life. How
could I not reject and push away and scream goodbye
forever at you and you and you? I had to. I had to spiral
into myself until I was inside my own organs all twisted
like that shriveled up kidney they took out of Jay's body.

But he also tells me things I do enjoy hearing: like how I've
paid my dues.

Transactional worlds are easy to understand.

Blue Hat

I pick up Jay's blue wool hat from my desk and move it to
the mudroom, thus moving it into a future I didn't think
would turn out this way. See, Jay doesn't pick up his own
blue hat anymore. Only I do. I am in the future now. He is
not.

I state the facts,

      but don't actually believe they're true. No.

Flight's delayed, meeting went late. I know this is common.
Happens to lots of people who lose a loved one. Shut up. I
don't want us to be like other people. We have magic on
our side. He might really come back.

Come here, let me show you something.

I open his closet door.

Smell that?

I breathe in his favorite words: pleasure, buttons, baby.
See? A message for me. A foreshadowing of his return.

Important

So many things unfinished and stacked like empty cartons
we keep by the refrigerator for eggs from the coop.

But Jay stopped collecting way before he died.

Instead, he did things like hold up Donald Hall's essays or
poems and say: *This is an important book.*

I wish I'd kept a list of all the important books. All the
clean sentences. Jay loved a short sentence, followed by a
long sentence, followed by a short sentence.

Time

I have lost my understanding of time. It's about proximity.
Which seems to be everything and nothing at all. Death is
death. Time doesn't change that. Time doesn't heal like
they tell you it will. I know they want to be kind, offer up a
positive in the midst of grief.

But please.

Time will heal, says the person at the post office when I
collect my mail. *It'll get easier with time*, says the hospice
worker who calls me every other day. Does that mean I will
forget a little bit more each day? I don't see how. I
remember every inhalation, every exhalation Jay took for
the three coma days. I remember how he twitched and
grabbed at the bedclothes,
>   how it seemed like he was reaching for me,
>   how I said, *I'm right here, baby,*
>   how the nurse said he didn't really see me,
>   (*it's just a reflex*, she said),
>   how I screamed *Get out of my house!*
>   And she left.
>   And it was just the two of us.
>   My head on his chest.
>   I think of it every day.

>   It never feels further away.
>   Time is not a measurement of distance.

But time is linear, they say, so if you move forward in time,
you move away from the past where the trauma is

positioned. Like when you travel away from Copenhagen, you leave behind the mermaid. Oh well that does make sense. Realistic. Sane.

Come on.

And anyway, why would I want to move away from the blue hat, the book of poems, the little notes Jay made me? Or even from the moment he died, the light, the expansion of an entire universe?

The events inside my life are happening inside of me, all at once, all the time. So there is no forward or backward in time. There is just this. To experience all of time happening at once, I believe, might be a way to travel interdimensionally. Not away from something like when you get on a plane and leave Denmark. But inside it. So then, loss is not lack. Because you never leave anything and nothing ever leaves you. So loss can fill a person in a different way. This is not an optimistic or positive-thinking reframe. No. It's just a sensation I'm having. I will write it down on a little note and maybe Jay will see it. You think that's magical thinking? Optimism? No. Optimism is a tenet of time. And I have lost my understanding of it as well.

> I guess some smart person would say
> that's a good thing. Shut up with
> more positivity. All I'm saying is
>> time
>> doesn't
>> heal
>> shit.

The Last Bar of Soap

I lie in my bed. I am afraid of nothing. My husband is dead. I saw him die. Right before my eyes. Right here in our bed. I used to be afraid of everything. Now I am afraid of nothing. I am half now. Incomplete.

The last bar of soap Jay made is on the top shelf in the bathroom. I stand on a pile of books. I can barely reach it, but I do. Then the books topple and I fall. I cry on the floor of the bathroom.

The soap smells like his hands.

I remember death. It's not the opposite of life. It's the opposite of warmth. It's separation. Separation cuts you in half. Leaves you cold. I hold the last bar of soap in my hands.

It gets smaller and smaller. Soon it will be gone. I watched love being taken right out of my arms. Now I am afraid of nothing. I lie in my bed. I dream of my halfness. Half that is gone, half that is left, half that can never be whole. Death is the opposite of warm. Death leaves you cold. But its light lingers.

Jay's Tallow Soap

Christmas, 2009

III

Slovenia, 2012

On the Train to Slovenia

I stare out the window of a quiet, empty train car with a small cup of espresso in hand. I am moving into a world of memory, though it is new to me. The world I am about to enter, this place called Slovenia, was a memory of Jay's, a memory called Yugoslavia.

He lived for a year in Ljubljana, the capital of Slovenia, a city of poets, and I picture a place where he sat in churches and dreamt about a girl he loved who didn't love him back. She had red hair and freckles like I did, but I was only ten back then when Jay was eighteen and writing love poems for the Celtic-looking Slovenian girl.

As I sit on the train, I anticipate a movement forward into my altered life, a life without my husband, and a movement backward in time, to a place where he anticipated what his life would be. In this place called Slovenia, maybe my foot will fall upon a sidewalk where he stood, gazing at the road before him, wondering if someday a girl would love him back.

Jesenice says the sign when the train enters Slovenia. And then I see it. I see what he saw, what he loved, what made him a poet. Romantic outlines of an unkempt abandoned shed, a wild meadow full of plants that do as they please, so different from the stark, clean, orderly lines of Austria. I see the hardened world of steel spread across a valley of worn-out ash trees in the undergrowth of the Karavanke Mountain Range, desolate and alluring at once.

Rail station after rail station. I think of our first date. He asked me if I liked borscht. I said yes and he brought some to my post-divorce, single-mom apartment over a soap shop in Vermont, my daughters away for the weekend. He smiled and impressed me with some Slovene words he'd learned long ago and we watched *Doctor Živago* in its entirety. After hours of lonely frozen Russia, I put my head on his shoulder. That was the night he told me about the red-haired girl and his life in the former Yugoslavia. I wished that I had been that girl, that I had known him when we were young.

I would have loved you, I said. And then, I did.

I have walked out of the bedroom, away from the house, away from the road, away from his clothes, his car, his soap, his silence. Ivo Andric's *The Bridge On the Drina*, the last book he was reading, on our bedside table. His glasses left on top. My body is unto itself, altered now without the things of Jay.

The train pulls into Ljubljana and I imagine walking to the center of the city, to a statue erected in honor of the national poet, Prešeren. I will stand in the shimmered linden tree shade, eclipsing reason and pushing me forward. The mantra in my head: *Where are you?*

I imagine myself walking the streets of a literary city, trying to catch Jay's breath in the hot air of summer. The light, obscured but present, moves across the sky over the Tromostovje Bridge. A piece of his past and my future, together.

Hotel Garni

A van for my literary group has been sent to the station to collect me. The others were picked up from the airport an hour ago, twelve students of poetry, some old, some young, some in the middle like me.

Hi, hi, hi, they all say when I climb into the van. We are taken to Škofja Loka, a hill town near the capital. At the small Hotel Garni, I have a single room facing the river because they know my husband has just died and are treating me with care. I let them. I appreciate the view.

After a shower, I change my clothes, put on lip gloss, but instead of going out, I collapse onto the bed. The shuttered windows are open wide with no screens.

I touch my body. In a few months, I will be so skinny, I will hardly exist. But today, I am all here.

An hour later, I venture to a gathering of poets in the center courtyard of the small hotel. They're a blur to me: a young man, another young man, another, a young woman, a middle-aged woman, another, an older woman, a middle-aged man—no one stands out. But they form a circle that allows me in, and I am held up by its structure. I love them for this, these faceless people.

The hotel manager gives us each a shot of apricot brandy before a welcome talk by someone I don't remember. They go to dinner together afterwards, but I am tired. I stay behind and sleep.

Shadow Wife

The bells of Škofja Loka wake me too early. They are loud bells, intrusive. I want to hear a beginning in them, as if my life is about to move forward, but I can only hear an end.

I stare at the ceiling from my bed at the Hotel Garni, lying inside the ending of a person who used to live in my body. The person I'm left with is indiscernible to me. She is shadow, all vapor. She moves without a body. Does anyone see her? There's a knot in the center of her solar plexus and this is what gravity clings to, holds her up, keeps her moving. But her arms and legs flail about. Look at her: a river creature, boiled on the shore of an ancient Yugo-Slav embankment. A shadow wife, she lives as I die.

Metamorphosis.

A wild untethering has occurred. Gone is everything known, everything sacred, everything I once believed in. So I just lie here, face up, on my bed in a post-Communist country where my beloved lived when it was part of a place called Yugoslavia and the capital was Belgrade, which is now just the capital of Serbia.

I look out the window at the Selscica River, green and muddy, think about the genocide in Bosnia down the road such a short time ago. I wonder if I can find the Drina and the Mehmed Paša Sokolovič Bridge in Višegrad. I wonder if I will even look. It's many hours from here. I don't know.

The church bells continue. *I need coffee.*

I throw on my shapeless black dress and scour the streets of this medieval town. I don't notice the cobbled bridge I cross, the stone walls along the river, the towering blue mountains in the distance. I don't look up at the terra cotta facades, the open shuttered windows, each holding a simple flowerbox that welcomes me with cheerful red carnations. I don't know that the red carnation is the national flower of Slovenia. Wait. Is it? Maybe it just looks like a carnation. I don't even care. I'm just trying to keep my head steady on my neck. *Coffee*, the only thought I allow in. The hotel breakfast isn't for two more hours. I need coffee now. I need it bad.

I don't learn the Slovenian word for coffee and I don't feel bad about not knowing. I can't move that far outside myself to ask what the word is. I just hope that someone will speak English to me. Not that I'll understand that either.

The morning holds sounds in my head, milling around in muffled confusion. Nothing makes sense. I won't get lost in this little town that will serve as the literary residency's home base, with day trips into the capital city, Ljubljana. Škofja Loka is easy, with bridges and squares and art stores and churches. The cafés are closed, but I spy a grocery store. It appears to be open. I hold up four fingers to the lithe Slovenian lady behind the counter.

Can you make it a quadruple?

I want to say to her, *my husband died six weeks ago,* because I want to be seen as much as I want to hide, long to

70

open as much as I want to withdraw.

Do you see this shadow wife?

But I don't say anything. Just drink my quadruple in practically one gulp, walk back to the Hotel Garni, cover my ears when the church bells begin again, look up at the wide sky, red-castled rooftops in the distance a blur.

The Poet-Guide

After a day of workshops, the unidentified fellow writers
and I eat a late dinner outside under a trellis of deep red
bougainvillea. For sure this is bougainvillea. I know
because someone just said it and I heard it plain out the
corner of my ear.

I order sweet sparkly wine and look at a menu full of words
I don't know. I wish I had my sunglasses to combat the
glare of candlelight. Everyone is talking, but I sit
imploding. What am I doing here? I want to crawl back into
my bed at home, the bed where Jay died. I want to push
that moment away and yet I cling to it. Maybe he's sitting
on the bed waiting for me. Maybe I just dreamt death. I
have to find a piece of him here. I will fall into madness if I
don't. Maybe I'm already crazy. The candlelight flickers. I
can't read the menu. I don't understand what the others are
saying, even though they are speaking my own language.

Don't look at the menu. What do you feel like eating?

It takes me a minute to realize that someone is speaking
directly to me. I turn to the Slovenian poet who, I guess,
gave the talk last night. I vaguely remember shaking hands
with him.

I'm sorry, what did you say?

*I asked what you feel like eating. You don't need to find it
on the menu. They'll make you what you like.* Got it. He's
asking me what I want to eat.

Honestly, I don't know what I want.

Yes, I can see that.

He stares with focused eyes, smooth and silken knife points, exhilarating and jarring at once. It surprises me. The abyss of Jay's illness and death has been so lonely. Until this moment when a stranger seems to see me.

Well, I guess I want fish.

Good. Get the river fish. We're surrounded by rivers. That asshole over there ordered shrimp. You order shrimp when you're near the sea. Here in Škofja Loka you order trout.

I stay inside myself at dinner, talk outside talk. Or at least I think it's outside talk. I always reveal so much of myself. I hardly know the difference sometimes between the inside of me and the outside.

My husband died six weeks ago, I say to the poet, whose name is Luka Vodnik.

Oh, I am very sorry to hear that.

He used to live here.

Was he Slovenian?

No, American. He lived in Ljubljana for the school year in 1978 and '79 on a student exchange.

Oh, I see.

Maybe you can help me find him. I mean, find where he lived or went to school.

The group will go to Ljubljana tomorrow. Seek me out when we have a break and I will take you on foot to some schools.

In that moment eating trout, the man sitting next to me is looking at the inside out of me and I feel seen. He is silent after our exchange and I am silent, but it feels like communication is still happening. Maybe through our breathing.

He is going to help me find a piece of you.

Faerie Wine

I walk with my literary group down stone steps to a restaurant on the Ljubljanica River, the hot of day alleviated by a shaded terrace. Luka orders small pitchers of wine for us all to share.

I don't say much to anyone. Don't feel I have to. The faceless group just allows me to exist with them. Quiet-like.

Try this, Luka says, pouring me a glass. *It's from Dolenjsko.*

Tastes like fairies made it, I think, but don't say.

Very beautiful countryside, Dolenjsko, he says. *Magical woods: forest chapels and shit like that.*

We eat trout and potatoes, drink more wine, then blueberry brandy. Then I see everyone standing up, but I feel like I've had too much to drink, though I haven't. Luka wraps his fingers around my arm as I stumble and almost fall. He catches me and I blush.

That wine was strong, I say, embarrassed. I see myself from the outside, a filtered reality. Is it a reality away from Jay? Or a reality toward him? I can't tell. But for sure, a reality taking me away from grief for just a moment. A reality encompassed in the river fish, the wooded wine spirit, taking away drunkenness and replacing it with some kind of opening.

The fingers on my arm seem to allow me to unravel. Touch. My eyes fill with tears. Luka sees them.

I stop him on the sidewalk. The others have disappeared from view. *I don't know what's happening to me,* I whisper over the sound of the street. He takes my shoulders in his large hands.

You're okay. It's going to be okay.   He squeezes tight.

I don't think so.

Kiss me, kiss me, kiss me, I think. But he doesn't. I don't want that anyway. Right?

On the bus back to Škofja Loka, I text my children. They remind me of who I am: soccer mom, brownie maker, caretaker. Not a person who loses control. Why have I come to this foreign country? I don't recognize myself here at all.

Beloved

My skin is moist under a yellow sundress as I walk alone.

I pass sculptors making giant birds from scraps of metal on
the sidewalk, then move through the farmer's market,
where I buy a basket of figs, green and sweet and hot.

On a wooded path, I scale the side of Ljubljana and, at the
top of the city, across a meadow of saffron crocuses, I see a
twelve-foot cross made of rusted pipes and giant screws.

I see the outside of images, slippery impressions, but make
no connection to the insides. I understand the name of
things, but not the things themselves. In this way, I walk
through a world of symbols. Only nothing means anything.

On the way down the narrow stone stairs, someone in front
of me stops short, turns fast, and I fall into him. I don't
move away. I want to be touched, to be held, to be kissed
and kissed and kissed. Break through the symbolic world,
make something real. Will the stranger kiss me? No, I don't
want him to. I'm married. But I do want him to. *Kiss me,
kiss me, kiss me!* A tiny moment, a split second of polarity,
spinning upward, my sexuality unleashed despite, or maybe
because of, the terror of death.

Oof, the stranger says.

I'm sorry, I say. He turns and smiles at me. I blush.

Kiss me, I think. *Kiss me.* He turns back to the path.

I try to walk the lines between vitality and death, all of which seem to be reflected in Slovenia itself, a country precariously positioned between antiquity and modernity, East and West, conformity and unrelenting freedom.

Suddenly it feels like hundreds of people are on the stairway. I ignore them and continue on, make my way back to Prešeren Square, eat forest berry gelato by the Ljubljanica River. I am dizzy with desire and misinterpret everything. I will begin to negotiate life through this new filter. Am I using a sexual force to draw people to me? To combat loneliness? I don't know. I don't know.

I see my group near the Three Bridges. Catch up to them.

What does Ljubljana mean? I ask Luka as we all walk to a poetry reading.

Beloved.

Beloved. Of course. I bite my lip to hold back a tear.

Are you here with me? I ask the sky, but there's just this: me standing on a street in Ljubljana, standing as half the person I used to be. Being half is nothing to judge, nothing to fix, no new understanding to come to. Half is just half, not better or worse than whole. It just is. It's just the state of me. I am half now.

Butterfly to Bosnia

The sun pulls my fragility from the broken tenements I live
in, along sidewalks twisted and sidewalks fractured. I want
to walk where he walked, place my foot in his footprint.

I move as if in a dream state of sorts, in front of cars, bikes,
as if I am unconsciously trying to find a way to get to him.
Deeper and deeper into the core of Ljubljana, the
possibility of Jay on every corner, just a moment of him,
please, somewhere on the hot rainless streets. I see a kiss
suspended on the edge of the sun. I reach for it, but it
shatters on the ground. I turn toward Luka. Did he see it
too? He looks right into me and doesn't take my hand, but
it feels that way, his fingers touching my wedding ring, two
flowers opened wide, one white gold, one yellow, a tiny
diamond in the center of each.

It's called the 'Butterfly' ring, Jay said when he kneeled
romantic-style by the woodstove in Vermont and asked me
to marry him. I pictured tiny blue-winged creatures landing
on my finger, drinking nectar from petaled sunshine.

Now my hand feels safer than it has since he died. It's
small in the imagined embrace which leads me across a
narrow bridge of cobbled longing,

> longing
> to catch a glimpse of anything that
> will wake me up from this strange
> new reality I live in.

I need to go to see a bridge in Bosnia, I say to Luka. *Maybe after the residency.*

Bosnia? No, no you cannot go alone.

I tell him about the bridge and Jay's fascination with it.

That was his dream not yours.

I want to yell: *Fuck you, you don't know me!* But I'm relieved to hear that I don't have to go.

The Devil's Bridge

I walk in front of the group in my red sundress, cross the *Devil's Bridge*, Hudičev Most, and am the first one in. Luka tells me to go ahead, the cave will come out to an opening on the other side. The Soča Glacier makes the air damp and I shiver in the drizzly chill.

Zadlaška Jama, the cave that inspired Dante's creation of hell at the beginning of the 14th century, has winding chambers and hidden levels. I clamber fast with determined feet and curious hands scaling dirt paths and walls. The cave is all around me, consuming. I breathe in cold air through my mouth and, very quickly, begin to feel disoriented as I move without heed or caution or regard for the unknown terrain.

Then suddenly, I am alone. And there is no more light. I can't see my own hands. I have no flashlight or phone with me. And I don't hear the others. Where are they? I stop walking.

At five feet three, my head touches the ceiling. With walls on either side, I reach in front of me and feel a slab of stone with indentations carved like elf stairs. I climb to a shelf landing. Maybe the way out is up. But, feeling the ceiling above, I realize

there's no way out.

I missed the sign that said: *Abandon All Hope, You Who Enter Here.* How quick I was to enter something so massively profound.

I abandoned all hope already, I say out loud. *There's nothing you can do to intimidate me. I don't care about living. Just take me, Darkness. Swallow me whole. Devour every part of me.*

I hear the screams of a million anguished souls. The sound controls. The sound pierces. It moves sideways across me, a bashing tone, though oddly ambivalent. Its weight lowers and pushes the ceiling to crush, suffocate, impale me with shards of rock.

GO AHEAD AND FUCKING DO IT!!

And then I remember:

MY DAUGHTERS.

No, I whisper out loud. I see the girls' faces, one with freckles, one without. *No, you can't take me. I have to stay.*

And then, in a flash, fear rises up through my body. I am alone in Dante's cave, alone in the slippery, low-ceilinged blackness. I can't move, frozen in a chasm of infinite grief. I feel as if I might die of my own terror. Why didn't I wait for the others before I went forward with such fierceness?

I am still, afraid to tremble, afraid of every beast enraged, a wild unknowable force, one I hadn't bet on encountering. It twists my breathing knot-like in my chest. Eyes wide in the blackness, insanity blowing cool subterranean air.

Love gave us both one death, Dante said. Where did Jay go when he was lifted right out of my arms?

I scream his name out loud in the cave.

You went the wrong way. I hear a low voice, see a small penlight. It's Luka. He climbs up the wall and sits close to me in the blackness. I can feel his shoulder touch mine. He tells me to turn around and climb back down.

I can't, I whisper on a breath. *I'm afraid.* I begin to cry. I can feel him looking at me, though I can't see his face.

Hey, he whispers. *You're going to make it out.*

He climbs down first. I wish he would hold my waist, the folds of my sundress in his hands, lift me off the wall, so light in his grasp. But he just takes one purple sneaker after another and places them where they need to go. Once outside, he and I stand together, looking over the guardrail, the ice blue water raging below.

I'm embarrassed, I say.

It's natural to be afraid in a situation like that. You had the true experience of Dante's cave. You went to hell and now you are out. He laughs. *It's perfect.*

But I'm not out of hell.

Well no, his voice turns sober, resolute, turning outside talk inside out. *There's no true way out of hell. We can't control*

84

shit in this world. But sometimes there's refuge in small moments. Moments when we find ourselves outside the cave.

Everyone keeps telling me 'time heals.'

Well, that's bullshit. Hell is hell. Time doesn't alter it.

Where is he? I whisper. Luka doesn't answer. We just look over the gorge, breathing warm air.

Communion

The bells of Škofja Loka wake me again. They lure me
onto the street in Slovenia and to the Sentajakob Catholic
Church.

I sit in a low wooden pew of the five-hundred-year-old
church, full of women in Italian dresses, purses clutched in
their hands each time they stand, my bag thrown carelessly
on the pew behind me. The women seem older than I am.
But they're probably not. There's so much I'm not aware
of.

I sit up straight, though, and imagine myself as one of
them, a wife again maybe, a different kind of woman than I
am. Someone with intentional dark hair and long slim
limbs, nails clean and painted red. I imagine that one of the
men across the pews will ask me to dinner—a fifty-year-old
divorcee with good teeth in a white linen shirt. We will
laugh and he will open the car door for me. I will marry
him by week's end. Yes. I will be a wife again. A different
kind of wife. One who is so so so so strong. She'd never let
her husband die. No.

Yes. I will have a well-ordered life. Everything will be
perfectly clear, precisely defined. The service starts and I
stand up with the other women.

But the icons at the Sentajacob Church stare down at me
from above, indifferent. The stone walls, cold. I realize that
I've been taken in. Duped. This is a place to offer your
faith? Faith in what? Desperation? Slicing the air, hoping to

find something in the cracks—A MIRACLE—to explain the cruelty, the suffering of life. I explored every trickster jam I could to cure the cancer. The winter before Jay died, I called the El Santuario de Chimayo in New Mexico to get a bit of earth consecrated by God—by Christ they said—known to heal wounds large and small. This little bit of magic came in a little plastic baggie. I put it on the legs that hardly held him up, smothered his swollen belly, and within weeks, Jay could walk again, the malignant fluid in his stomach gone. Everyone said it was the chemotherapy and maybe it was, but I was sure it was Christ.

A month later, he was nauseated and couldn't eat. I watched him being wheeled away from me as I sat in the hospital chair, a familiar place. I used to meditate while I was waiting in the hospital. I'd repeat the mantra of my ashram days, *Om Namah Shivaya, Om Namah Shivaya.* But I had stopped chanting. Too tired. Thoughts came into my head and I forgot them. That time was like a secret, its alleys turned inward, complex, spiraling, a maze undone. They gave him an IV and soon, he stopped vomiting and could eat a little.

I took him home. Lifted each swollen leg up stairs to a metal walker inside the front door, then stayed with him as he moved slowly to the bedroom, pushing along the hardwood floor to bed.

All the things in life he enjoyed were over. Wrestling with boys, basketball with girls, tending chickens, cooking dinners, baking bread and his favorite thing, memorizing poems, the latest had been Emily Dickinson. It came and went in spurts, this reciting, this remembering. He spent hours on her poems, a postcard next to our bed of her wide eyes and words on his lips:

> *This is the Hour of Lead-*
> *Remembered, if outlived,*
>
> *As Freezing persons, recollect the Snow-*
>
> *First-Chill-then Stupor-then the*
> *letting go-*

Kelley, he said to me early one morning with a clarity I had not heard in a while.

Yes, my love.

Jesus was here.

He was?

Yes, he sat in that chair there.

What was he doing here?

He told me he was mad at me.

Why would he be mad at you?

I didn't show up for Gethsemane this year.

I'm sure he knows you're sick, I said, though I didn't know what to say. The books about dying I kept hidden under our bed spoke about people having visions of God or Jesus or angels when they were close to death.

He was mad because I'm just lying around every day. But I told him I'm mad at him too. For all of this.

Good, I thought. I was glad he was mad. I was mad too. I went outside, the deck lifted off the mud-filled land of a Vermont April, the sky bright with moon. I slammed the farmhouse door and screamed at Jesus,

Stay the fuck out of our house!

I am waking while dreaming, the incense wafting through the air as I walk toward the Renaissance-era alter made of black marble for communion. I don't know what makes me go. I kneel, open my mouth as I see others do, an archaic means of transfer. When I return from the bread and wine, I notice the women in my section, none of whom went for communion, glaring at me, shaking their heads in metronomic unison. Maybe they can see me hating God as I walk down the aisle, the wafer dissolving in my mouth, ready to be pissed out, the arrogant God I once loved mocking me. I want to scream at the women, ask them how they can sit tailored and curtailed, conservatively clutching those ugly leather purses.

I leave the church. I wander faithless, unmade, over Capuchin's bridge, past the town coat of arms. Church after church through the streets of Škofja Loka. A moving spiral. Open your mouth and start again at the top. Around and around. You can't get out. Fall into a gutter. Fall into the river. Bones grind themselves together. The priest eats leftovers. No sign of resurrection.

A Day in Škofja Loka

I don't notice the cobbled bridge I cross, the stone walls along the river.

I don't look up at the terra cotta walls, the open shuttered windows, red carnations. I wander lost, unearthed, through the square, past the stone fountain. I wander ravaged, in the smoldering heat.

The taunting, rainless, vulgar day.

I eat trout by the river.

And trout by the river. And trout by the river. Dead. You are dead.

Metelkova

I stay in Ljubljana longer than my group and stand alone under a streetlamp, waiting for the last bus back to Škofja Loka. I search for a euro, and a poem tumbles out of my pocket, unfurling an ancient Slavic sound, gentle whispered citadel. I catch it. Then a kiss drops from somewhere. Outer space? I watch it break into a million pieces on the cobbled street of Ljubljana

and sweat runs down my leg even though it's evening. There is no escape from the heat and I sink into unbearable pleasure on the bus.

I feel death reaching its hand to me from the future, I whispered to Luka earlier at the artist enclave, Metelkova, where the prison-turned-youth-hostel held a poetry reading. *Even in the most beautiful moments.*

Death is always happening, always here.

It hurts.

Life is suffering, life is hell. So what can we do? We must relish the moments of pleasure. Like listening to poetry
and drinking whiskey
and being consumed in the summer heat.

Painter and Poet

I'm late. Inside the small hotel lobby, someone directs me to a closed door. Carefully, I open it. Everyone stares. I've interrupted the famous poet, Tomaž Šalamun, and his wife, the famous painter, Metka Krašovec. They are talking about the color red. I slip into the back and try not to breathe or make a sound.

I use red in my paintings to see what red can do, Metka is saying. *I listen to it. I try to hear my paintings speaking to me, a presence that wants to be materialized.*

As we listen to Tomaž Šalamun read from an English translation, *On the Tracks of Wild Game*, from his collection, *Po Sledeh Divjadi*, I notice a new person in the crowd who looks to be around thirty-five-ish, a small, grubby, scruffy man with a tight black t-shirt that says, Živjo! with a big X across it. I know what this means. Or at least I think I do. Something like: *Don't say hello to me, you fake fuck.* I laugh.

After the reading, people mill around drinking wine for thirty minutes before walking to Metka's gallery in the alley near a pizza place I will frequent regularly three years from now when I move to Ljubljana for nine months.

But right now, the alleys and cobblestoned roads blend together in flashes of images and sensations. I write words in my journal: hot, sweet, sweat, post-communism, then see the man in the black t-shirt and walk over to him before the group departs the Hotel Mrak.

Hi, I like your t-shirt.

Hvala. Thank you. I am Vid.

I am Kelley.

Do you like the poetry of this asshole?

Šalamun? Do you think he's an asshole? I thought he was a very famous poet.

He rode the backs of capitalists from the West who corrupted our country. That's how he got famous. His poems are shit. Don't you agree?

Oh um, I don't know. I can't say.

But you just heard him read. You liked it? Well, you're from the West, so what can I expect?

I wasn't making a critique in my mind about whether I liked it or not as he read. I was just taking it in. Being open.

You should always be making a critique of everything.

Why?

Because vapidity causes suffering—maybe not for you personally but for humanity. You have to think about that.

One of my faceless literary friends comes over. She's

blurry, but I hear her say: *Who was that?*

Someone who made me feel like a stupid American.

Here's to us, she says, raising her glass to mine and we sort-of-laugh, then make their way with the others to Metka's gallery.

I stand in front of an enormous painting of a blue forest. At the parting of the trees, there is a small girl in red by the edge of a lake. I fall into the painting, submerged in the color blue, feel myself free in its darkness, dislocated from my body, free even from memories, slam, slam, slam. The portal lures with color.

You like this one. Luka Vodnik has come up behind me. He is hearty and full of life, but his voice is low, pointed, intimate. He wraps it around me like a large flat tongue. I shiver.

Yes.

The group surrounds us then and someone says: *Are you going to buy it?*

Years later, after hearing about the death of both Tomaž and Metka, I will regret saying no. A lost opportunity to look endlessly at something I could dive into and drown.

Leaving Ljubljana

The Croatian Line screeches into the Ljubljana train station
as I pull apart from the post-Communist platform, the thick
smell of capitalism luring me back into my real life.

Goodbye, my comrade in hell, Luka says and hugs me
goodbye.

I board the train and whisper: *It's time to go.*
I didn't find you.

I've slept alone for eight weeks. Up until the last week of
his life, when Jay was too weak to hold me, I spent every
night nestled in him, my head on his chest, long arms
around me.

I'd like to have a king-sized bed, I'd said to him years
before.

No way, Baby.

Why not?

*In a king-sized bed, you'd be too far away from me. You'd
have your own life, your own dreams way over there and
you wouldn't be curled up in my arms so close every night.*

The outline of Austria outside my window lulls me to sleep
and I pretend his arms are around me on the train and I'm
sleeping in the embrace, my own dreams spilling like

glasses of whiskey, sweet sparkly wine, countless bones of trout.

Jay, I whisper out loud. *I have left Slovenia.*

I close my eyes, feel his hand on my face, curl up into myself, my memories and his memories left behind in a place of poetry, scorching heat, and the shade of the linden tree. The train carries me altered, the beginning I thought an ending, indeed an ending, an ending opened wide, fallen and swirling.

Maybe you're at home now, waiting for me in our bed. I look out the window at the Austrian night sky and make a secret wish. I feel embarrassed, exposed in its articulation, but I wish it anyway. I wish *for God*, in all bitter failings, on each painful breath, in the wide expanse of my heart, to come back to me. *Please*, I utter, but don't forgive. All the stars of heaven,

unreachable.

IV

Iceland, 2012

I Follow the Books of Poetry He Gave Me

"And the traveller hopes: let me be far from any
Physician. And the ports have names for the sea,
    The citiless, the corroding, the sorrow."

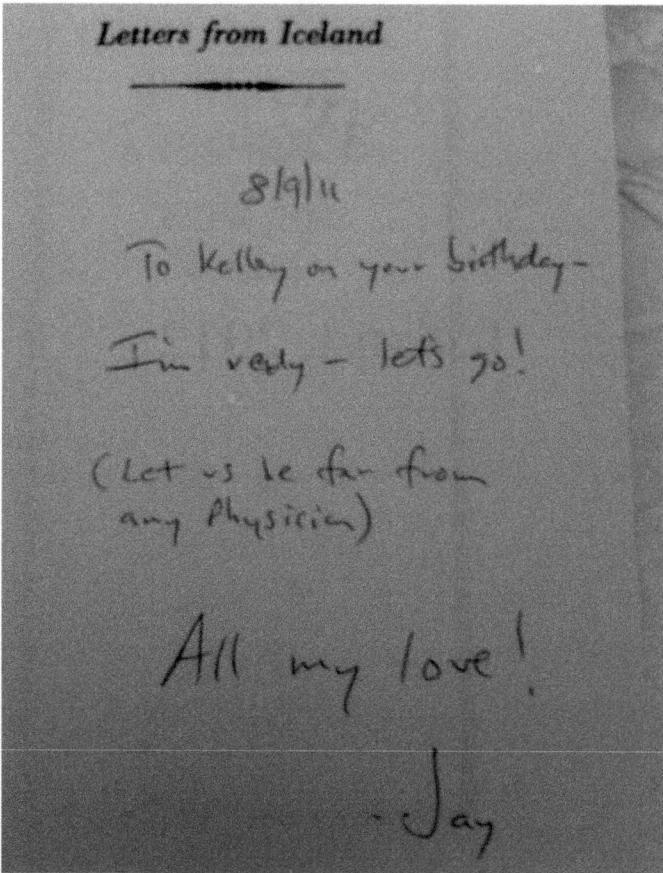

Letters from Iceland

8/9/11

To Kelley on your birthday —

I'm ready — let's go!

(Let us be far from
any Physician)

All my love!

— Jay

like Auden's *Letters From Iceland*

A Free Pass

Your mother questions the logic of going to Iceland in
winter. But you don't care what she, or anyone else, thinks.
You do what you have to do to survive.

Sometimes you drive past the house on a back-country road
where your husband first kissed you. You sit in front of its
blue shuttered windows and replay the memory over and
over again.

Sometimes you to shop online with life insurance money.
You spend $1000 on lacy things you'll never wear. *You're
crazy*, your mother says. *You're going to run out of money.*

Sometimes you do errands and tell strangers about how he
died. Sometimes you stay locked in your bedroom, drapes
drawn, blankets over your face.

Sometimes you convince your best friend, Krista, to fly to
Iceland with you. Krista saw him dead—so she doesn't
question your state of mind.

The two of you land on a floating volcano, a world where
ash is made into tiny earrings only faeries can wear.

You will buy violet dresses made of gauze, drink cold
vodka, whisper long-voweled love words to cats on the
street.

Having a dead husband gives you a free pass. It's a pass
you give yourself. And when you do, you have to take it.

From Askja's Window

Branches on the trees outside my window at Askja's little house are bent sideways as though the wind has blown them that way and they have remained horizontal.

To remain horizontal sounds good.

Krista and I found the little house in the center of Rekjavík on Air BnB. I used the name "Kiki" on the website application. It was Jay's nickname for me. I wondered if the house really belonged to someone named Askja or if that was a nickname too. But I loved this Askja when she picked us up at the bus station and the way she called me Kiki and the white vinyl jacket she wore over a pink chiffon dress.

The sun has barely risen by eleven in the morning.

> *You would have loved the low light. It allows sadness.*

> Yes, the impenetrable relief of melancholy.

Sundhöllin

I sit for hours in the most extreme heated water I can
withstand, while ice slices pummel my wet hair and I
notice that tears don't freeze like in Vermont. They just fall
and swirl into steam. I sit in my grey bikini with pink roses
and hear him.

I knew you'd love Iceland.

Krista joins me in the water. She is exactly my size. We
have the same color hair. Mine curly, hers straight. She
wears a one-piece. It's black.

Armors my soft.

The Icelandic Artist

The artist, Oddur Eggilsson, doesn't seem to like me. He's embarrassed because the Lutheran priest, Bjarni Olafsson, brought Krista and me to his apartment without calling ahead. So underwear is drying on plastic racks in the living room and there is nothing to offer his unannounced guests: no brennivín or wine or vodka. I feel bad, say maybe we should go.

No, no, says Bjarni Olafsson. He brought us here for a reason: to dump me with the artist so he can go off with Krista.

We all sit on the couch and talk. I tell them I signed up for Elf School.

I can't believe you buy that shit! Oddur Egilsson yells out. *People who try to sell tourists on that are just interested in taking your money. Only fools believe in such things. The only thing in life that exists is beauty.* He stands up abruptly and shows us his paintings—on the wall, on the tables, in piles against the closet door. I like the solemn rain scene on a dark day.

We call umbrellas 'wind shields' in Iceland, offers Bjarni Olafsson, glancing at Krista, then at me. He is nervous and has rabbit energy with a big round head and frog eyes.

I like this one, I say. Still, the artist is gruff with me. I ask about the light behind the sky. He shrugs the question off. I wonder why he dislikes me.

After thirty minutes of looking at paintings, Bjarni and Oddur leave the room, talk in hushed tones from the kitchen.

Hey Krista, let's get out of here, I say.

But then the men are back. I notice that the artist has a changed countenance toward me. I look at the priest, who is looking at Krista. I am uncomfortable and go to the bathroom. When I come out, the painter is in the hallway.

You are very beautiful, he says.

That's just a dead husband in me you see, I want to say, but refrain. I think how trite he is, how shallow, commenting on something so fleeting, so subjective. I'm not a static object, not up for interpretation. Still. I've been trained to accept complimentary remarks about appearance as flattery. Even though it fans an ignited rage inside.

So I say: *Dante saved the eighth circle of hell for flatterers. He deemed flattery to be worse than murder. I won't tell you what the punishment was.*

I'm not a flatterer. Just an artist who enjoys beauty.

Yes, of course. Well, thank you, I say, back in line, dutiful to the societal norm. *I think it's time for me to go, though. Thank you for having us.*

I would very much like to paint you without your clothes on, he says.

Jesus Christ.

That is very kind of you, I say as I self-loathe.

Will you come again?

I'll have to see.

Well, take my card, the artist says, as he rummages through a glass bowl on a shelf near the front door, finding a tiny red piece of corrugated paper. He hands it to me.

Here.

I take it from him, smile, then notice that Oddur Egilsson seems strong. Maybe he could pick me up in the air and place me just where he wants for the painting. I start to imagine his hands on me, smoothing my skin out till it's flawless, pounding sadness into something taut. I like the idea of being painted naked. It's thrilling. I like the idea of being bent over the sink where he makes me wash his brushes. I imagine it as we stand in the hall.

Kiss me, maybe I want to say. I could say it right now and it could happen. *Fuck me.* That could happen too. Would happen.

But I hate the selfishness of the artist. He sees me, but not Jay. He sees my body, this body that is full of life, while my husband's body is ash. *It's Jay you see, not me!*

My husband and I were two of a kind, I say to the artist and put on my pink wool hat, black winter coat, tall boots. I turn myself into an elfen cat and slip onto the night street of Reykjavík.

Wax Gnomes

Krista and I walk up four flights of stairs to get to a small apartment in a sea of buildings near the University of Iceland, surprised that the librarian is able to fit six people around a small wooden table in the center of the kitchen. Wool sweaters dominate.

It's a relaxed evening, but when everyone leaves in one big flurry, including Krista with the Lutheran priest (through whom we got the invite), I wind up alone with the librarian in the kitchen. Piles of dishes. Ceramic double sink. Empty wine bottles.

I'm a little tired. Would you mind driving me home? I ask the librarian, as he and I stand in his tiny kitchen. He's blond, in his mid-forties. Through his loose green turtleneck, I see the shape of a man who may have been fit in the past.

Would you like to have another drink with me first?

Thank you, but I'd really like to get going, I say.

He pauses for a long time, seems to be thinking deeply. I look at the pictureless refrigerator door, the wicker basket with three old bananas. Bulb of garlic.

I would like to see you without your dress on first if that would be okay.

I want to be the kind of person who could say, *Give me a*

fucking break. But I'm not her. So I just say, *No, it's not okay* and wonder why men keep saying these things to me. I'm not used to it. Maybe it's the Viking way.

He just stands there looking at me. Then he puts his hand on the blue wool of my hip. I don't move. He doesn't move.

If you won't drive me home, it's okay. I'll call a cab, I say softly, and remain in his hold.

I glance into the living room. There's a sadness in the way the furniture faces the curtainless windows. I imagine him sitting on the couch, staring for hours at the vast expanse of Iceland. I imagine him wandering through the rooms of his apartment, running fingers along dust-covered books of poetry, a wish of sorts, something long forgotten. For a second, I think maybe I should let him undress me. Maybe it will make him feel better. But no. No. I can't. *I have to use the bathroom,* I say. He doesn't loosen his grip. But I'm not afraid. Not of him, not of anything. *Let go.* He does. I step over a pile of faded white towels on the floor by the toilet and look in the mirror. I don't know anything about the librarian's sadness, but I know that mine has made me fearless.

Jay looked at me over the candle at Pane E Salute, an eight-table restaurant in Woodstock, Vermont. It was our third date.

One thing you should know about me, Kelley.

What's that?

I suffer from depression. You should know that.

I don't care about that.

You should consider it. I'm a bit broken. You're so bright, so alive. You should think about it. Maybe read about clinical depression.

I took a sip of my fragile pinot noir, ate a bite of trout, watched tears roll down his cheeks.

Thing is, we were both broken when we met. He suffered from depression. I suffered from anxiety.

Would you be angry if I didn't get on the plane? I whispered to him once as we stood at the Southwest gate in Terminal E at the Boston airport, about to take a trip to visit his brother in Boulder.

Of course not. You need to do what feels okay for you.

I'd been taught in my new age upbringing that if I *meditated* while in the air, and *focused my mind* on a safe landing, the plane wouldn't crash. Really. I actually believed that. I felt responsible for the flight, which created enormous anxiety. And sometimes, I didn't think I could do it. I was terrified of the control I'd been told I had. So I watched Jay board the plane to Boulder without me.

When he died, my fear of flying ended. Completely. In fact, most of my fears ended. Because I realized how little power I actually have. What a relief to acknowledge this truth.

Sometimes Jay would sit silent for hours, staring out the window. *I know it's beautiful because you've told me what the light looks like*, he would say. *But I don't see it.*

It's okay. You don't have to feel anything at all, I'd say and curl up into him, trying to understand this thing called depression.

He held me through the night, assuring me that the pain in my chest was panic, not a heart attack. I told him I would love him no matter what he accomplished in a day, no matter how sad he was or how long he had to sit in that chair. He told me he loved me even when I made him take the back roads because I was afraid of fast cars on highways. He and I were two sides of sameness.

Some days, when no children were around, we would lie in bed and he'd read poetry to me. I would close my eyes and dream we'd be together forever, dream I'd always be safe, dream our children would love each other and we'd be a full family. His boys would teach my girls how to tap maple trees and my girls would teach his boys to sing arias.

Jay, I whispered in bed, the light moving slowly across the sky in the February afternoon, three months before he died.

Yes, my love.

You're going to get better. I know it.

Baby, he said, *you're going to be okay if I don't.* My eyes swelled. He took my hand, put it to his lips. *You've gotten so strong, my darling. You aren't afraid of anything anymore.*

Only because I'm with you.

No, there's a life inside of you that's dynamic and unafraid. It's you. He touched my face. *You've made it possible for me to face my own self—the ugliness of depression. You've shown me what beauty is. Your relentless love— it makes you the bravest person I know.*

This is how I was loved, I say out loud to myself in the librarian's bathroom and draw cat whiskers on my face with black eyeliner from my purse, tighten long blond ponytails into ears, stand on the toilet seat, look at my emaciated body in the mirror.

You know, don't you, I say to the librarian when I return to the kitchen. *That my husband died seven months ago.*

Yes, yes, I know that. Oh, I'm so sorry, he says, shaking himself out of a sort of stupor. *I'll drive you home right away.*

Thank you, I say.

112

But might you walk with me tomorrow?

Maybe, I say, but know I won't.

He drops me at Askja's apartment. I stare at the ceramic puffins in the pantry, make myself a cup of tea, but don't drink it. I feel a tremor in the room, a volcanic heat, a rattling of Christmas dishware.

I say out loud:
> *My mind cannot control things.*
> *There are no airplanes to keep in the air,*

> *no men to cure.*

I put my coat back on and walk and walk through a tunnel of wind along the streets of Reykjavík—past shops of ash pottery and phallic murals, down to the seafront, and across to the cul-de-sac filled with tourist shops of Icelandic sweaters and gnomes made of wax.

Baby!

I love you.
I kissed your hair.
You didn't wake up.
I will think of you
all day until I see you
tonight.
All my love,
Jay.

Red

Krista and I sit in the full theatre wearing black clothes and heavy eye makeup, watching a violent piece by the Icelandic Dance Company, a ballet based on fragments of Norse mythology. When the performance is over, we follow the crowd.

They're going into another theatre, Krista says.

Seventy-year-old women in tight mini dresses and leopard heels, young women in polka-dotted tea coats and knitted caps, men in skinny jeans and black sweaters are funneling into a different theatre.

I think it's a play, but we don't have tickets, Krista says.

Fuck it, let's sneak in, I say.

I love this version of you, she says and squeezes my elbow.

We find two folding chairs in the back of the intimate space, not knowing what kind of a performance it will be until it begins: a two-person play in the Icelandic language.

I think it's about Mark Rothko, the painter, I whisper to Krista. I recognize his paintings on the stage. And though we don't understand Icelandic, we are moved by the emotion the performances elicit.

Let's go meet the actors, I say to Krista as the theatre begins to clear out.

I think the signs say 'keep out.'

I don't fucking read Icelandic, I say.

Try to keep your personality like this, she says and laughs. *It's the real you.*

Is it?

We ignore the keep-out signs and go backstage to meet the actors.

You brought us to tears even though we don't know Icelandic, I say to two actors. *It was the authenticity of your emotions that made us cry, like when poetry moves us even when we don't always understand the words intellectually.*

The older man says thank you. Then kisses Krista on the mouth. The younger man and I blush. Probably for different reasons. I'm blushing because I know how pretentious I sound.

The Lutheran Priest

Krista and I eat at the Lutheran Pancake Supper in a
suburban part of Reykjavík. Bjarni Olafsson, the priest,
invited her to play the guitar at the church. We all sing
together while she plays. Then we eat thin, light pancakes
at the church supper with old women in white woolen
dresses and tiny blond children in Scandinavian cardigans
with metal buttons. Bjarni leans over to Krista and speaks
quietly to her. She laughs out loud. Later, she tells me that
he asked if anyone had ever put an egg up her vagina. And
that he'd like to.

Krista's brother died 5 weeks before Jay. Is she filtering life
through her sexuality too? Like I seem to be? Nah, men
have always liked her.

On Laugavegur

I eat white confection on narrow streets in Reykjavík, drink
things that burn, let faeries paint me tangerine. You're too
young to be a dead poet's widow, they say.

You don't believe me?

I'll dig up his bones. Place them in a row on your porch.
Look how white they are, how perfect, how strong.

You still don't believe me?

Look at my mansion on the hill, blood and guts outside the
door. See them writhing, hear them wailing. Don't put them
in the compost. Nothing will grow from them.

I think I see you. I always do. You there, is it you? It must
be you. I feel your hands on my waist, pulling me close. I
catch my breath. But it's not you.

It's a yag goblin with jagged teeth. His mouth is up my
skirt. I scream.

The Icelandic wind laughs at me then slices my cheek in
half.

I will climb carefully on steadfast rocks, wear tiny dresses
made of gauze, drink rose colored vodka, whisper love
words to birds.

I will crawl through the streets of Reykjavík, turn myself

inside out, offer this version to giants in the night. They will chant Nordic spells and I will fall backward, into outstretched arms. Who could help but catch a raging faerie? They stand in line to offer words of consolation.

V

Italy, 2013

Ghost Embrace

Another writers' conference. My bed at Le Sirenuse has a white embroidered quilt and faces open doors to the sea. Warm air moves across my body. I lay still, staring at a white-tiled ceiling. My hands move above my head as I pull him to me from another dimension, then move my hips from side to side, imagine the weight on me.

> At home I found one more bar of soap he made from beef tallow. It was wrapped in brown paper. I didn't open it, but put it in a box on a shelf lined with pink silk. Sometimes I took it out and put it near my face.

> Cloves.

In Italy, I walk with my new friend from Brooklyn who tells me I'm

> *joyful for a sad person.*

> *That's the dead in me,* I don't say.

She and I drink limoncello with groups of poets. I buy linen dresses for Claire and Lily, then ride on the back of a motorcycle with a novelist from Asheville along the Amalfi Coast. I laugh/scream with absolute delight.

Italian waiters and Sicilian artists lean into me against stone walls on stairs to the Tyrrhenian Sea. I press hard, then join the larger group. *I'm sorry, I can't.* Doesn't matter when my husband died: six weeks ago, six months ago, a year, two, ten. He's dead. I look normal on the outside, a fully-formed human. But I don't exist at all without Jay. The entirety of who I am is drawn out by the narrative of loss.

Come here. Come here. Don't touch me.

Giaportia, Says Calvino

It's crowded, but no one's there. Not even your beautiful
children. Just you moving in the sunlight, you moving over
bridges, you turning with canals. Only the dead could make
something so beautiful. The sight of it is your own self.
Your own resurrection is possibly occurring. Little by little.
Maybe.

But you feel the alchemical shift in your blood. The dead
stare at you, glisten in Adriatic sunlight. The others mean
nothing to you anymore. You're glad they're not here now.

You'd have to look in a mirror, make yourself beautiful.
You'd have missed everything.

All that matters is the dead: whispers of the dead, breath of
the dead. The dead inside your very self. Your very self
feels the dead slide up close.

You touch the heart-shaped locket that holds his ashes. It's
been months since you took it out of its box. You wonder
why you did today.

The soprano sings with a single cello in the church. A
stranger sees you cry. Your cries make her cry too. The
whole of your heart, acknowledged.

I brought you here so I could finally die, you hear him say.
Even though he died already. At least that's what you
thought happened. It's not like you just heard a rumor. You
were there when the light flooded the bedroom and stole

him up, up, up. The wake of an incorruptible moment.

Years later, you'll eat pizza in a covered boat with your
children. Patterns of water, thinly spread for miles and a
promise kept, spoken directly to the Adriatic: *I will never
let you go.* In this way, there is protection. There is no
betrayal.

You'll have a little dog too. The girls will feed her crust on
a white leather vaporetto seat. And everyone will watch the
city floating.

PART TWO

VI

Montreal, 2013

Rue de Saint Paul
(Montreal One)

I don't ask Graham about his life. I know he's not available.
I don't ask him why he's here in Montreal with me, why
he's traveled so far to see me. I think he lives in California.
I don't know. We met on a poetry website when we both
commented on a line-break we liked. I tell him about Jay. I
talk endlessly about Jay. He reads things I write about Jay. I
know he's not available. I know. Listen, I said I know. I
don't care, okay. I know he's unavailable. I know. I don't
care, I said. I just, I don't know, I just love him. *I love you I
love you I love you I love you.*

Graham allows Jay to exist even when he squeezes me tight
and whispers hard into me, *You're mine,* as if he's holding
all three of us in his arms and this all three of us are safe
there inside a corps of vulnerability. My therapist calls this
mental construct *triangulation.* But Graham welcomes the
part of me that can't separate from Jay, allows him in,
allows me to be as dark as I need to be, lost in grief, half
dead myself and Graham's own halfness (for reasons I do
not know) battened full to mercy, a moment in time, raw,
lost.

We walk the grimy streets of Montreal from Chinese
noodles to beer bar one, peche mortel, and beer bar two,
none of that fancy shit. Miles and miles of black slush
along the sidewalks, crushed cans, used condoms, goop and
talk about our narcissistic stepmothers, our love of
fragments, travel anxieties, fear of snakes. Spit, splatter,
gravel, gum.

We walk at the same pace, each step moving closer to each other and each step further away, but always walking with a purpose. To understand something about ourselves, the dimensions of intimacy, where the boundary between two people exists. I lean against him in line at the Botanical Garden, as we wait for the butterfly exhibit. His body gives me something life cannot.

Graham mitigates the cold.

Sometimes we ride the rubber-wheeled metro train. This stop, transfer, that stop, tomato-egg dumplings, plié and stretch, movie theatre, opera house, drip, drop, detonated destination. We watch a Finnish ballet performance at the Place Des Arts, stand close at intermission, share a ginger ale. He pushes his thigh between my legs, takes a sip of soda, his hand on my lower back. I don't ask him about his life. I don't ask why he's there with me, why he traveled so far to see me. I just put my head on his chest. *This is the beginning of my body unfolding into someone other than you.*

A few months later, at a sample sale in New York City, I buy a red chiffon dress to wear the next time I see Graham.

The dressmaker asks: *Do you have a man?*

Someone else in the shop asks: *Or some kind of significant other?*

No.

Well, you will, they both say and loosen the ties around my bare breasts.

But when Graham tells me he has recommitted to his girlfriend (his baby mama, he says), I cry hard and give the dress to my friend, Jenna. She says she'll wear it on the trip to Paris she's taking with her sister. The women in the NYC shop were right. A few months later, Jenna falls in love at Les Bains.

Rue de Saint Pierre
(Montreal Two)

I pack for an overnight trip to Montreal with a new
boyfriend. He lives on my road, Broad Brook. In the yellow
house Jay loved.

We drive north from Vermont to Canada. I sit in the
passenger seat with folded hands. I want to be perfect for
him. Every hair in place.

He thinks I'm pretty.
But I'm ragged to the core.
I think he wants perfection.
But he just wants to be loved.

So here is the tragedy.

Inside this new relationship is that which can never be
realized. Separation is occurring as love is unfolding. It
opens into a wide expanse before us.

*

I look out the window of his black BMW with my stupid
blond hair and think I see the person I was right after Jay's
death, which was only a year ago, yes, there she is:
someone who didn't mold herself into anything other than
exactly what she was in the moment: cat, elf, warrior,
faerie, truth speaker.

Fearless.

Now that I'm with this new man, I'm afraid again. Of what? Afraid he will die too? Or just leave? Cold at the bus station like Graham did? Graham who was never mine, but I made mine in my mind.

I spiral, then

                shut down.

It was here in Montreal where Graham allowed Jay to exist along with him. But there is no place for Jay in the BMW. Is there?

Then oh so tenderly, Montreal Two asks: *What's wrong, my darling?*

Here, in the light of Christmas coming, its red and blue baubles on the streets of Montreal, the frigid wind blowing down filthy sidewalks, I feel myself crawling back inside the memory of being separated from love. It rises up in my chest as I sit in the warmest, safest place I've come to know: the place next to this man, his hand on mine, this man who seems to love me (who says he loves me), a man I vowed fidelity to, secretly in my heart, the late spring day I met him, at a neighborhood party. Pot-luck. We connected over our Leo birthday discovery, August 8 (him) and August 9 (me), one day (and ten years) apart.

But there is a sense that he is leaving me as he comes near. I can feel it as slush splashes on the car.

*

131

Want to get something to eat?

I nod.

This part of town used to be a walled city, I hear him say as
he parks and we get out of the car on the narrow street of
Rue St. Paul, walk through the drippy melted snow,
cigarette butts swirling in grey run-off. We see a bird
struggling to withstand a stream of gutter water in the
street. This new boyfriend stops and picks the small bird
up, places it in the shelter of an abandoned courtyard. We
are both silent. I am too moved by his gentleness to speak.
And anyway, if I did, it would be a blood-thirsty plea. I
don't want him to see my desperation. No, not even one
hair out of place.

We make our way to Bocata, a cozy wine bar with exposed
wooden beams, dim candlelight, antique books on the
shelves. I soften my eyes.

> In the future, I will take note of what lives on the
> land of this man's yellow farmhouse: evergreen,
> burdock, grass, ramp, fox, fisher, mink, raspberry,
> woodchuck, black bear, maple tree, coyote,
> butterfly, bat, rabbit, deer, birch, chipmunk, red
> squirrel, grey squirrel, mouse, bobcat, dog,
> goldfinch, bluebird, robin, hawk, owl, jay,
> hummingbird, bee.
>
> I will look even more carefully and notice the things

he's planted and cultivated: striking bee balm, reverent monkshood and the flowering crabapple tree, Weeping Louisa. I will notice what he chooses to plant. Brilliant red, widespread span, broad and bare.

He will reveal himself through the care of weeping trees, offer the smallest creatures a tender touch: baby chicks, tiny seedlings, little dog. So much is understood through observation. Cultivation. Encouragement. Luscious peonies. Blooming lemon trees.

But my plea will dangle.

Dangle.

Dangle.

Don't ever leave me, I say, as restrained as possible, and put my head on his chest while we wait for a table at Bocata.

Don't be a silly goose. I never will.

Fuck you, I know you're lying.

K-
Surprise!
I'm still
thinking of you
from coffee through
to hip hop,
Spruce and
Teak.
I'll
buy groceries.
Call me. All my love —J

Paris in High Tops

The possibility of life with Montreal Two reminds me of a long time ago, like when I got to talking to this dreamy Danish boy and we made out all night on the boat across the English Channel from London to Calais. He said I was unlike any girl he'd ever met, which I took as *maybe this is love.* But then my stuff got stolen at a youth hostel in Paris, which didn't really upset me too much, except that his number was gone with my jeans. So I walked along the Seine in lacy white high-tops and listened to Jacques Brel on my pink walkman, then through the Tuileries, where my father had sailed toy boats in the fountain while his mother, my grandmother, taught at the Sorbonne. I borrowed a bike from a friend of a friend, Dmitri from Brooklyn. I loved the way my long curls whipped through the hot Parisian air with no helmet. I imagined never leaving France. *Coming here was a great idea,* I told myself. And even though I had to keep washing my one pair of underwear in the sink each night, I was happy. When a French boy I met, Pascal was his name, climbed over a stone wall with me and into the jardin of royal colors and we drank wine and kissed, I thought about how great ideas like love can push you into your future, into the curation of a person you imagine yourself becoming. It was so romantic to become someone who is becoming. All imaginings possible.

Hope continues to be my coping mechanism even though I intellectually understand its predatory impulse. That sneaky fuck called optimism, a delusion I continue to propagate.

VII

Slovenia, 2015

Portrait of a Poet's Square

I sit on the steps of the pink Franciscan church and look out at Prešeren Square. Six footpaths and two bridges lead away from the square. No cars allowed. An inhabited place, lively, but not over-crowded.

I'm back in Ljubljana because I got a Fulbright fellowship. I applied last year but didn't make it to the second round. An American poet friend told me to reapply. So I did. I'd started a second Master's degree by then and the Fulbright committee at Dartmouth College read my application and called me in for an interview. After that, they recommended me to the U.S. State Department. I made it to the second round this time and the application was approved by the American government. Then my work got sent to the U.S. Embassy in Slovenia for final approval. When some old friend in Vermont asked, *How did you get a Fulbright?* and I told her the phases of application, she said,

Oh so you knew someone.

> The accordion player, in his heavy green cotton pants, pushes and pulls to make his arcade music. I wonder how he sits in the sun for so long. A blond-haired, gelato-eating family of five seem to be speaking a Germanic language of some sort, maybe Dutch, maybe Danish. Their speech is

subdued, quiet, heartiness tempered
by the swell of scorched air.

No, I didn't know anyone.

I begged Montreal Two to come with me. *Or least make a commitment before I go?* Because I love you I love you I love you. But he couldn't come, he said, and he wasn't ready for a commitment.

Let's see how it goes when you get back, he said.

You mean in nine months from now?

I'll come and visit, he says. So.

I'm alone.

But not.

But am?

But wait.

I am in between.

As usual.

I can't move forward.

I have to wait here on the bridge.

A child screams in the square. A mother in a sheer red dress scoops the child up and kisses him. Her limbs are brown and thin. She dances to the accordion and the child begins to laugh. A group of tourists pass. The tour guide speaks a Slavic language of some sort. I can tell it's not Slovenian. Maybe Serbian, maybe Croatian.

I look up at the statue of Prešeren, the most famous poet of the land, who lived a long time ago. I can't remember when. Behind him is his muse, a lovely mermaid, holding her arm out over his head. I wonder how many women Prešeren saw in this form. Did he have one muse or many? In this moment, I don't hear the accordion. In this moment, the warmth of the day is turned inward. I feel the heat as part of myself, not something to buffer from the outside. I think about being someone's muse. It's intoxicating. This intoxication, in turn, becomes the muse for *me*. It always happens in this way.

Teenage girls in cotton dresses ride by on bicycles with pretty baskets and tassels. They ring the bike bells shaped like dragons and butterflies. Some plain metal. They must be tourists because dragons are everywhere in Slovenia. So many local girls together would not have bought dragon bells. Or would they? Three-Dragon Bridge is right there. I can almost see it from the steps of the pink church. Stone heads fierce. A mosquito lands on my arm. Smack. Miss. Maybe I will look up Luka Vodnik.

I continue to look at Prešeren, think about how my muse is always myself as someone else's muse. My work is affected by the effect I have on the other, just as I always see myself in relation to someone else. I rarely stand alone.

This is not a modern thought, it's not politically correct. A person is supposed to be whole in them/him/herself, independent of another. Inspiration should come directly. It should not come from being viewed from the outside, no matter how close to the inside of you the viewer is.

A group of gymnasts make a pyramid in the square. Each drop of sweat lands on another.

A ballerina comes on pointed toe from behind the Prešeren statue. A violinist plays for her. Their duet is the sum of my thoughts. I am my own muse now. I have to be.

It's a moment in time that is altering me. Ladies with leather bags pass and a juggler kicks his leg high when I hand him a dropped beanbag.

I'm on a Fulbright. I got it because my application was strong. I did it on my own. I am my own muse, my own critic. Please self, assume the role of sovereign. It doesn't matter that you don't know anyone. You will. All of time is happening all the time. Even in this moment.

A moment in time when wind doesn't blow and sun burns skin and the wide expanse of sky hovers over this square only, on this afternoon, with no one but me to see it. Or maybe Jay sees it too. I don't know what he sees anymore. I don't know where he is. The café across the river to the left of the dragon bridge is chaotic. The café to the right of the dragon bridge is raging. The whole world is here.

Castle Wedding

Autumn produces a quickening. It happens while I sit here
minding my own business and learning that it's not called
hot wine, but *cooked* wine, and so I have to say *kuhano
vino*. When something is cooked it revitalizes your organs,
not just warms them up for a moment. So the quickening
happens while my organs respond to the slow dance. I
mean I'm just sitting here on the steps of the castle.

Look, Luka Vodnik says, *some country girl is getting
married in the castle. All the country girls want to get
married in the castle.*

Where do the city girls get married? I want to know
because I am a city girl, *was* a city girl, so does that mean I
will never get married in a castle?

You're already a queen, what good will a castle do you?

Later we go to the coffee shop in the Faculty of Arts library
with stone walls and he tells me that making a poem takes
your own pure strength of being, word by word, and I tell
him that when I used to perform in plays, a director who'd
worked with David Mamet once told me that the strength of
who I am is enough

     just say the words one by one and Luka says: *Yes.
Who you are is the whole world.*

Ljubljanica River Walk

Sunday mornings are quiet on the street by the Ljubljanica River.

I have a little dog now. She and I walk slowly. We hardly pass a soul. My boyfriend, Montreal Two, bought her for me. It's confusing. He moves toward me, then pulls away. I cry about him all the time. Tell Luka on hikes up mountains. Tell Krista on What's App.

A pile of debris is floating in the river. As it moves closer, I see it's a human body.

A police officer comes over to me and asks a question in Slovenian and I say I don't understand, *ne razumen*, and he walks away.

My therapist says that every small loss after a big loss can often be even more painful than the original loss. Is that why his dismissals make me feel insane? I don't know.

The face in the river is covered in mud. The knees and chest cavity, perforated and swollen. I stand silent. The policemen on either side of the river stand silent. No one moves. We watch as it floats under the bridge. I bow my head when it goes by. My mind is still. A man is dead. Death comes in a flash. I think about people who don't grab what they love when it presents itself. Take it and devour it.

Maybe he doesn't love me.

I stand so still by the river. The body is floating slowly. Silence is broken by the sound of sirens. A man in scuba gear jumps into the water. He pulls the body closer to the dock and six large men try to pull the body out.

Dead bodies are heavy, I think.

I remember when the man from the funeral house came to carry Jay's body out of our bed and into his long black car. I asked my friend, Mary, to come and be with me. Her husband insisted on coming too. I was glad because his help was needed to carry Jay's body out. *Dead bodies are heavy*, I said to Mary on our Vermont deck in early May. Dead bodies are heavy.

Changing Flats

I have a dream where all the toilets are stopped up and a
pipe bursts and scalding water burns my hand and a giant
sun-globe shreds my eyes and the water level rises and I'm
about to drown and there are those weird giant Slovenian
river rats (coypu?) floating all around me and I don't know
who to notify because the man who owns the building
      is my boyfriend's friend
      and this makes me feel funny about it.
      And I can't call my boyfriend
      because I know he won't help me
      because he doesn't want his friend to feel bad.

This flat or that flat—they're all the same. The toilets rage
in each. My stomach hurts no matter where I am. I think
I'm awake, think I'm going to the bathroom,
              think I'm tripping on a pile of
              expensive clothes.

Anyway, it was just a dumb dream I had in my apartment.
And only dream-me would use the British word *flat.*
Dream-me is pretentious as fuck. Which I'm only now
beginning to realize.

Wedding Dresses

Here I am again, standing outside the bridal boutique.

When I walk my little dog along the Ljubljanica River in the mornings, I'm too embarrassed to stop, afraid someone—a wool-capped man or green-scarfed girl—might notice me looking at the white sequined swaths of taffeta. So I only turn my head quickly for a glance at the shop.

But on the darkened street at night, I stop, place my hand on iron-ribboned bars, peer in. There's always a light shining on the white and ivory-colored dresses.

My Yorkshire terrier has gotten used to the routine. She sits on the cobbled sidewalk in this antique city and waits.

I often feel ridiculous, a woman over forty with mostly grown children staring at wedding dresses, but somehow, I can't turn away. Perhaps as I stand there, gazing at the shelf full of shoes, the shimmering satin slingbacks, the darling white-laced pumps, the glittery gold Mary Janes, I am reminded of the lost youth I have started to feel as I anticipate my daughters becoming women. But that's not the reason I look in. No, that's not it.

I stop because I long for the construct of permanence, for love to be actualized in a promise. *Please marry me.* It torments me as I gaze at the sequined bodices, the lightness of silk, the strong swaths of taffeta, but I can't turn away, I can't turn away, I can't turn away.

Somewhere Near That Castle Everyone Goes To

You need some comfort, Luka says, and takes me to his
mother's village, his mother's house. No one has ever lived
in it, but it feels like home. He knows his way around the
kitchen. Or at least it seems that way. But I don't really
know because I am in the other room, staring at
photographs of his family. Gazing at the pieces of him.

His hands on the teabag make me cry. *It's rose tea. Has
vitamin C.*

Maybe I will ask him to touch me now and then: *Will you
put your hand on my arm?*

What's the harm in that? Once he picked a piece of lint
from my sweater.

VIII

Prague, 2016

The Dormitory

In Prague, everything careful is undone.

We enter cathedrals and cemeteries, faiths not my own,
faith nowhere I can see, actually. Does anyone see in the
crowd of cameras and selfie sticks?

     (And yes I was here and yes I was here and yes I
was here and oh yeah, you were here too, get in the picture
what are you doing over there, paying for another toilet
your stinking 5 crowns, 10 crowns? Every pee more
expensive than the last.)

I pick up an unwashed sweater and pair of old jeans off the
linoleum floor of the dormitory. *i like how you're messy,* he
says.

Kava

In Prague, I drink črni kava velika—that's Slovenian for big
black coffee—but the letters are all mixed up on the
machine, scrambled into Czech. Still, I know what it says.
Because Slavic and Slavic and Slavic.

I know all the words for coffee now and this makes me
stand out less. I try to only open my mouth when I know at
least some variation of some Slavic word. I want to blend
in, to merge, to feel no separation.

I carry plastic cups of črni kava upstairs before anyone's
awake. The sun comes into my room and onto the linoleum
floor. And the whole world rushes up through me.

Bernarda

I have traveled to Prague with a group of Slovenian poets.
One has become my movie star friend. I call her that
because of her sunglasses. Which is dumb. But she laughs
and I laugh and we are the same, except for all the words
we don't understand, her being Slovenian and me being
American. She calls me kutiš, which means something like
sweet, and we drink beer at breakfast and buy tiny trinkets
for Luka to pin to his vest and we all move at the same
pace. Bernarda is short like I am so everything slows down
for us.

Unbearable

In Ljubljana, we are on one side. In Prague, we're on the other. In Ljubljana, we use euros. In Prague, we use crowns. The exchange place by the border of Austria and the Czech Republic is too expensive and so we still have pockets full of euros.

A thing from the other side.

In Prague, there is lightness and there is heaviness, or so the story goes, and I always wondered whether I was light or whether I was heavy, but in Prague, I know how the pushing down of the world can lift you like when you jump on a trampoline with someone else and they send you flying.

David Černy

I google David Černy while standing under his giant
sculpture of Sigmund Freud hanging by one hand out a
window, a comment on the uselessness of intellectualism.
Here's his pic on my phone: subversive gaze, thick black
hair, maybe around my age. I can't tell for sure. The sun is
fierce on Staré Mesto and my sunglasses distort the image.

I see another Slovenian friend, Anja Kos, slight, cropped
black hair, coming out of Švejk U Zeleného Stromu with a
cigarette she was sure someone at the bar would give her.
She smiles and holds it up triumphantly.

Anja Kos and I walk to the Futura Gallery, where two giant
torsos, sixteen-feet high and bent at the waist, are plunged
into an outdoor wall. I climb a ladder between the legs of
Černy's sculpture, *Brownnoser.* At the top, I peer into a
giant white asshole and see a video loop of former
president of the Czech Republic, Václav Klaus and
ex-director of the National Gallery in Prague, Milan
Kinzak, feeding each other porridge while Queen's "We
Are the Champions" plays. The porridge spills and the
characters keep at it. As an outsider, I am aware of my
ignorance, know that I don't actually understand the current
political situation in the Czech Republic, soon to be
Czechia, but I think I get the point: those in power stuff one
another in excess.

I take my head out of the asshole and see Anja Kos
standing at the top of the ladder at the identical sculpture

next to mine. Anja Kos is completely still, taking in the video for quite some time so I put my head back into the asshole and continue to watch the loop. Maybe there's more to consider.

At the Poetry Festival

He brings me a glass of red wine while I stand outside in
the Prague air away from the smoke and too many words
spoken in too many languages I don't understand. Poems
translated from Slovenian to Czech and Czech to Slovenian
and everyone laughing when someone says *Americani*

                              (which happens a lot).

He knows he can't let me go back to the dormitory alone,
even though it really is okay, don't let me be a burden,
don't let me limit your experience, I can make it home
alone, I can find my way it's okay it's okay,

but no, because he knows right from wrong, but more to the
point,

he knows where I stand in relation to him and where he
stands in relation to me and he knows the appropriate
course of action because of this even though I don't know.
But then when it happens, I see all the wrong courses of
action
                              by comparison.

Everything's moved to the other side.

Modern Art in the Czech Republic

Giant babies made of bronze, each going its own way, and Bernarda tells us to go on in without her. Behind Kupka's swollen moon, he snaps a photo of me. *I like looking at you when you don't know I'm looking at you.* That's when I start wondering if he maybe loves me. Though there've been a million other signs.

Like when he took me into the Slovenian doctor's office and showed them where it hurt. It's not something to explain. Not even here in Prague. It's not love like what you're thinking. It's not of this world. It's formless. It's a giant creature from outer space or prehistoric times who pulls you up out of the abyss. It's that kind of love. Alien.

The gallery room faces the Charles River. He says *you are protected. There is someone in the other world looking out for you and someone in this world who stands behind you, no matter the distance.* The guard in the museum tells us to stop taking photographs. *I wish you would touch me,* I want to say, *put your hand on my waist.* But I don't.

Bernarda is waiting for us outside in her movie star sunglasses and we go into the museum gift shop and she tells me to buy the white ring made of glass baubles.

IX

Slovenia, 2016

At Čompa Drinking Red Wine With Luka and Discussing Nobodydom

Being a nobody should be your highest ambition.

What do you mean?

You think you're on a bridge, an in-between, nothing's settled. You're waiting for him to want to be in partnership with you. But a nobody shouldn't care about bridges. A nobody is self-created. Free.

But I love him.

Then love him. But remember, you're a queen.

A queen's a somebody.

Not your kind of queen. You're a nobody kind of queen.

I don't feel like a queen.

That's because you've placed yourself on the bridge. You're waiting for someone else to say you have a right to exist.

I'm not!

You are. And I'm not sure why. I will tell you this, though: Jay knew how to be a nobody and why it was important.

How do you know Jay knew that?

I know him.

*I've always wondered if you may have crossed paths with
him when he lived here. 1979. Before Tito died.*

Probably no. I know him because I know you.

On the Handlebars of His Bike

Get on my bike, let's get some food, he says and carries me
fast through the streets of Ljubljana on the handlebars of
his bike, my yellow dress fluttering.

I scream out loud with laughter, forget my life, forget what
I lost, what I can't find anywhere in this city of poets.
Forget what I want and still can't have.

We stop at a rustic bar with deep booths and eat sardines,
drink beer. I squint my eyes, try to make out my life,
yearning through words illumined and words invigorated
by life, life invigorated by words, words haunting, raw and
unbending, exposing more and more, and revealing,
opening into something that feels like love until I am
unwound, breathless.

I am relaxed from the beer, get back on the handlebars of
the bike and we ride fast through the city again. I'm not
afraid, weaving in and out of people playing saxophones in
the square, mimes and people turned upside down in
carnival cages by the river.

Biking in Red Heels

I ride my bike across Ljubljana in red heels, as I follow
Luka on his bike. We are on our way to the U.S.
Ambassador's house for a gathering. They said I could
bring a friend.

The chain comes off my bike as we cross Tivoli Park. It's
about to rain. I stop and shout. He comes back to me. *Fuck*,
he says, but fixes my bike.

I don't have a tissue for his hands in the tiny silver bag
across my chest, just my apartment key, Slovenian
identification card, five-euro bill and chili pepper lipstick.

The U.S. Ambassador reaches out to shake hands, but Luka
holds his up, grease-covered, and says, *I need to wash.*

I laugh and tell the U.S. Ambassador the story of the
broken bike. I tell it as though it's a story I've held in my
pocket all the years of my life so that I could one day stand
in the capital city of a post-communist country and relay it
to a U.S. Ambassador. I tell it like it's always been here.
Here in my pocket. A story that binds me somehow to a
gesture, a fixed movement, happening backwards in time
and forwards in time at the same time. How is this an
alteration of my relationship to melancholic optimism?

Later, when we ride back through the park at night, I will
ask Luka about that. And we will recall Slavoj Žižek
getting off the same plane that my daughters were on when
they came to Ljubljana. Then we will split paths at H&M.

Cake

I don't know why I've waited so many months to do this, but I ask Luka to drive me to the apartment building where Jay lived when he was on exchange in the former Yugoslavia.

I take a wrinkled envelope out of my bag, an old letter Jay sent his parents in 1979, and punch the return address into my phone. We drive to the outskirts of Ljubljana.

That's the building, I say, pointing to a communist-era apartment complex across the street. We enter its lobby, walk up stairs, and more stairs, looking on all the doors for the name of the family Jay lived with.

No success. We return to the lobby. I locate the family's name on a small metal mailbox among at least a hundred lining the walls. Luka writes a note in Slovene to please call him regarding an American boy who lived with them more than thirty years ago.

I can't believe they still have this apartment from 1979, I say as he writes.

Apartments are valuable.

The family lived in the countryside and didn't tell the government that the uncle who lived in this apartment died. So they were able to keep it for their kids who used it as a home base while going to a Ljubljana high school.

Common. He hands me the letter and I put it in the mailbox.

Jay walked on these floors, I turn and whisper to Luka.

I know. I know he did.

Luka and I leave the apartment building, sit next to each other on a wooden café bench, the center of Ljubljana loud and peaceful at once, the river speckled with light. He orders a piece of lush creamy yellow cake to share, four flights high.

Kremšnita.

Hvala, I say. Thank you. Then I imagine arms around me, holding me selfless, holding me tight, holding me star-like, luminous, breathing into my unlatched transparency, saturated stillness, everything summer. I am coming to life through the penetration of an inward gaze. It's here in the ether.

Do you think Jay sees us here? I ask Luka.

No, I don't think that.

You don't?

Jay is not somewhere else looking at you. He is inside of you looking out at the world, looking out at me. He wonders what this crazy old Slovenian tour guide is doing spending so much time with Americani Fulbright scholar.

I know what you're doing for me, what you've done.

Yes, yes I know you do.

Hvala, I say. *Hvala so much.*

Najlepša hvala.

Najlepša hvala.

A bit of Jay's past and my future, but mostly my future, settles here on the wooden bench as Luka picks a piece of lint off my sweater.

Najlepša hvala.

The Devil's Bridge II

I thought I'd feel a sense of melancholy on the rainy day in the foothills of Triglav National Forest. But I don't. My daughter, Lily, is with me and our little dog, Beesly. And, surprisingly, so is my boyfriend, Montreal Two.

Maybe he wants to be with me after all. I don't know. It's still not clear. I want total merging, to feel some sense of permanence in an impermanent world. How ridiculous. Nothing is permanent. But I love you. I love you. I love you. I love you. I love you.

We sit in the mouth of Dante's cave, but don't enter the portal to hell. I have learned well. I will not abandon hope. Look at me. I am dressed like someone who can properly take care of herself, a person who can navigate the elements. I don't go tearing into caves, down winding wet paths anymore. No. And Tolmin Gorge, Tolminska Korita, the site of Dante's cave, seems different. So I must be different too. Right? I am no longer weightless, moving along trails, across bridges, Devil's and others, on tip-toe, barely noticing forests around me. It's true that I've gathered the kind of substance you find when you are relentless about facing your reality—even when you wish you could float away like a fairy in a sundress.

So there's that.

The terrain becomes difficult as we wander along uneven and slippery trails in the woods, but silence creates comfort. There's no sense of going back and there's no sense of moving forward. There's just this moment. I see white stones in the forest. Blue river.

Light between the trees.

this is where *Cobbled Bridges* used to end

but

too
bad

it

just

couldn't.

X

Iceland/Home,
2021

Midnight Sun

In Iceland's second largest city, I study the map to understand my position. Akureryi is close to the Arctic Circle and I am wearing a winter coat in June.

I rent a car because I feel like it, and drive to the small town of Dalvik. At a farm between two mountain roads, there are giant blue eggs, black-speckled and exotic. I buy a bottle of sweet wine, then make my way to the sea.

The air bnb host, Swany, is tall. Tan. Her button-down is crisp under a turquoise vest. When she shakes my hand, I feel the weight of her gold and sapphire-heavy hands.

She shows me around the cliff-top property. A rustic barn is filled with paintbrushes in lemon-colored pots, twigs in striped candy containers, dried flowers

       hanging from wooden beams.

What else?

Black stones. Giant feathers. Orange swirled candles. Slide projector. Books. A mannequin wearing an apron. Cylinder woodstove. Hot tub.

Swany shows me to my modest room, then looks me hard in the eye. Wait. What have I told her? I don't remember. She seems to know.

168

Now, dear lady. My late husband, Pétur, wrote a book before he died about

metasophics:

> *how to die a spiritual death.*

Weird.
I just picked the place because of the view.

But my eyes swell. Swany hugs me and we step outside.
The air bnb sits at the edge of Eyjafjordur where
snow-covered mountains surround the sea and meadows of
purple lupines spread out all around the white wooden
house. I didn't know there would be a dead host luring me
to his meditation spot on a cliff above it all.

Swany shows me the path to take, points to it from the
driveway, *look*, beyond two hills of green grass and brooks
of cold clear water.

You'll find a circular hole in the ground, she says, and I do,
and an earth shelf carved out and holding a black ceramic
urn. I place fresh flowers in a glass vase. An offering. I sit
alone high above the sea. I don't know for how long. Time
is nothing. The sky is bright all night.

I ask Pétur to take his hand.
I ask Jay to take his hand.

Protect him, I say to them. Though I don't at all know what I mean by that.

I just know that I have another husband who is dead.

Gjallerbru

Dagny, the tarot reader at the Museum of Prophecy in
Skagaströnd, says that I stand on Gjallerbru, the bridge in
Norse mythology, which leads to the underworld. It is
thatched with glittering gold. *You are Reith, a horse-rider,*
traveling in the world, traveling in your mind. You are a
portal. You help men cross. In a way, you are their bridge.

Last time, I would have said, *fuck you, prophecy.* But not
now.

Now, I open.

Accept all possible explanations for this absurdity.

Because the car starts or doesn't start, the traffic's thick or
not, the chocolate's bitter or my coat is heavy. I can't tell
what is what. I have a mouth full of words only I can hear.
Data is hard to organize. A thing is seen or not seen. I
cannot bear to say his name.

Twice: peaceful in my bed, violent in the hospital.

Turn off the florescent lights!
I screamed at the nurse.

Then sang Grateful Dead songs into his ear, tender
husband of two years, Montreal Two. I pushed the

tube with my tongue and kissed his mouth, placed
my cheek against his. Then screamed again. They
asked if I needed a pill to calm down. I quieted
myself so they wouldn't throw me out, rubbed my
tears on his face. I love you I love you I love you. I
will not say your name.

Now I retreat to the unseen. Inside an Arctic wind tunnel. A
more comfortable vantage point. Here, I growl, claw, say
cunt with loose lips.

The tragedy within the romance, the feeling of him leaving
as he came near:
                        actualized.

We made beautiful love less than one week before a
stomach pain took him to the doctor on a Saturday
in November and they realized it was advanced
pancreatic cancer (*the worst kind of all*, Lena from
Sweden had said) and they did an emergency
operation

            and he died 38 hours later.
            On Monday.

The nurse escorted me to the front door of the
hospital, handed me a bag with his clothes, his
shoes. I walked into the dark parking lot alone. Got
into his car. Drove the windy backroads of Vermont.

Hung sheets on the windows in the yellow farmhouse. Turned off the phone. Curled into myself.

Don't bother me, anyone, don't bother me. Don't you dare bother me.

I got rid of the house on haunted Broad Brook Road, and didn't leave the apartment I retreated to in Providence from November to May.

Six months later, I got invited to an artist residency in Iceland. So I gave up the apartment and went. Because I didn't at all know what else to do.

Look, you are the Queen of Swords, Dagny says as she places the painted Tarot card down on the red velveted table at the Museum of Prophecy. *You protect others.*

Are you joking? I haven't protected anyone.

Sacred Marriage

I make very little indentation in the air around me, as I walk
and walk and walk along the paths near the sea, in the hills,
with bright orange poppies. I lose interest in food and grow
very thin. Consumption disgusts me. I become friends with
formlessness, moving through the world as myself, untying
threads that have bound me to identity, to the desire for
attachment to another person.

After what I've witnessed, isn't it normal to feel that
striving for the form of love is futile?

The expanse of love, though. That is another story.

Formlessness

I walk miles and miles in Skagaströnd for weeks and weeks
from one side to another. The landscape is tilted and angled
differently now and I am becoming comfortable in its
distortions. I force myself to learn new navigational skills.
Rewired brain. There is no recovery, only alteration. So I
become more and more mercurial, slip inside crevices and
peer out, get a good look at the unbearable, watch it, see
how it threatens and hovers, observe its tricks, become
smarter, then walk again out in the open, able to mitigate
volcanic terrain more easily.

As I walk, I ask silver foxes to help me not need so much
from the incarnations of love.

I ask arctic terns: *How do I embrace groundlessness?*

I ask puffins about impermanence.
There's no other way to be saved.

      The only thing is to unravel.
                        Again and again.

      cat, elf, warrior, faerie, truth-seeker

Release II

At the bottom of Spakonúfell, mountain of a prophetess, the orange-footed oystercatcher who has been calling to me every day on my walk, makes a long low sound, different than I've heard it make before. It circles away with other birds instead of returning to my path as it usually does. Then the light intensifies, and I feel a release. Kind of like when Jay was lifted out of our bed almost ten years ago.

Since this death was sudden, I wonder if maybe it has taken him longer to *transition*. That's a word people use. Into what, I don't claim to know. I don't claim to know anything. But I use these thoughts to self-soothe.

Those who are dead belong to me. No one can take them. They are mine to interpret, to defend, to wrap around me as I please. They come alive in moistness. I know the sensation well. There's nothing like it. The dead don't expect anything in return. They just fold me into air each night and my body becomes weightless. Vapor. The dead give themselves fully—because there is no them to give. It's something beyond them, nourishing. A hand in the dark.

I Have Worked Out the End of Civilization

I did it by being some kind of whacked-out high priestess. You don't believe me? I don't care. I give no fucks anymore. Giving no fucks is my superpower.

I walk through the streets of Akureryi, sit for a cello recital at the town hall, suck in the energy of those I have loved in the past and those I will love in the future. All of time is happening all the time. Inside this moment, inside of me.

I sit in a meadow of tall grass, ask the water that moves fast to the sea:

> Did I only live in the yellow farmhouse because Jay wanted to roam its halls? Did my dead husbands need each other? Are they Wonder Twins, activating a power that now pulses inside of me?

No answer.

So I get a cat tattoo and ride an electric bike through the busy streets of Reykjavík as holographic dimensions shift around me.

In Akureyri, there is a bridge floating between two pieces of a whole. I snap a photo of it. It's so small. Doesn't seem possible that it's real. Maybe an elf made it just for me. To let me know that love is not too far away. All I have to do is step through a stargate on the other side. And let go of a

hundred hardened ideas about the convention of
relationship

and shape of the spiritual.

Because God unformed, is a
much more palatable idea.

I take long walks near Icelandic horses who speak so
sweetly and all the flowers jangle and giant ferns jingle and
resurrection is occurring. My being takes nourishment from
nature, from light, from a world that radiates inside me.

It's a new age being born in my body. Not the capitalist
kind of new age that takes your money and gives you empty
lines like all you need to do to cure cancer is create a
compelling future and imagine a disease-free body,

and the worst line of all: "there are no victims."

Because there are victims.
I know two of them,

one swift at love and slow at death,
the other slow at love and swift at death.

This new kind of new age is a playful puppet theatre of the
absurd. The end of civilization is the beginning of radical
joy. It lives beyond rational thought. Because how can the
mind make sense of this madness?

All that can exist is a place beyond the dimensions of logic. It's outer space. It's nobodydom.

There is no Luka Vodnik here in Iceland, no guide. No one I imagine holding my hand. But I understand now. I claim my sovereignty, my liberation.

Najlepša hvala.

Hobbit Hill

After Iceland, I go home to the States and see my grown
daughters, one on the East Coast and one on the West
Coast. I follow Claire through the coastal forest of Hobbit
Hill in Oregon, down a tunnel trail of washed-up crab
shells. On the beach, fog obscures giant sea stones and it's
hard to see the horizon. Doesn't matter. Claire and I hike
until we are saturated with moon roses and faerie lore. We
drive back to the city of Eugene and talk to Lily on
Facetime in the car. The three of us laugh about something
silly.

The Red Dress

Later in the summer, I find my red chiffon dress in Jenna's closet. She says, *Take it. It belongs to you.*

I try it on. It fits. I snap a selfie of myself lying on Jenna's bed. Then look at the dress in the photograph for a long time. Dream of its new life.

Nothing is certain. I know this well. But I am becoming comfortable with the dissolve of expectations.

People ask me why I seem so happy.

Happy? I'm not happy.

There's an energy about you, they say. Like in airports and shops, and at the market, the cafe. *Joyful.*

I don't say, *That's the dead in me.* But it is. It's all of this. It shines out of me. It's atmospheric and interior at once.

It's love.

About the Author

Kelley McKenna is a 2015 Fulbright Grant recipient in creative writing and literature. She has an MFA in creative nonfiction from Vermont College of Fine Arts and an MA from Dartmouth College with a concentration in poetry. She is the Artistic Director for Foss and Moss Puppet Theatre of the Absurd, a poetry research project, which she began in Skagaströnd, Iceland, 2021. She is from Brooklyn, NY, and her Fulbright/selected publications can be found under the name Kelley McKenna Rossier.

Acknowledgements

I gratefully acknowledge the late Dartmouth College professor and poet, Gary Lenhart, for nominating the seed of this book in its thesis form for the 2017 Byam Shaw-Brownstone Award. This book would not exist without his belief in me and in the form of the *short*.

Thank you to the editors of the following publications in which these works first appeared.

River Teeth: "Taking An Art Class"
Dartmouth Literary Journal: "The Clothes I Wear"
little somethings press: "Warm Sauerkraut"
Dartmouth Literary Journal: "On the Train to Slovenia"
River River: "Communion"
River River: "Alone"
Apeiron Review: "picking green beans with lily"
River River: "Giaportia, Said Calvino"
River River: "A Day In Škofja Loka"

Thank you, Slovenian Literary Council, the U.S. State Department and the Fulbright Commission, for giving me the opportunity to live abroad in a global literary world—and thank you to American poet, Richard Jackson, for suggesting I apply for the Fulbright in the first place.

Thank you to Vermont College of Fine Arts, especially Robert Vivian, Laurence Sutin, Patrick Madden, Rigoberto González and the late Richard McCann.

Thank you to my teachers and advocates: Ann Hood, Dani Shapiro and Susanna Sonnenberg.

Thank you to the ever-brilliant writer, Ben Langston, my stellar editor, colleague and dear friend.

Thank you to Slovenian poet, Iztok Osojnik, mentor extraordinaire.

Thank you to Alison Huff, who kept watch.

And finally, thank you to John Reinhart and Arson Press for believing in this project and helping it come to fruition.

In the end, this book is dedicated to the memory of

Jay Rossier and Brad Atwood.

Citations

Alighieri, Dante, and Robert Pinsky. *The Inferno of Dante: A New Verse Translation*. Farrar, Straus and Giroux, 1996.

Andrić, Ivo. *The Bridge on the Drina*. University of Chicago Press, 1977.

Auden, W. H. "Journey to Iceland." *Poetry*, vol. 49, no. 4, Poetry Foundation, 1937, pp. 179–81, http://www.jstor.org/stable/20580684.

Dickinson, Emily. *The Poems of Emily Dickinson*. Belknap Press of Harvard University Press, 1998.

Kierkegaard, Søren, and Bruce H. Kirmmse. *Fear and Trembling: A New Translation*. Liveright Publishing Corporation, 2021.

Kinzie, Mary. *The Cure of Poetry in an Age of Prose: Moral Essays on the Poet's Calling*. University of Chicago Press, 1993.

Malabou, Catherine. *Ontology of the Accident: An Essay on Deconstructive Plasticity; Trans. by Carolyn Shread*. POLITY Press, 2012.

Steiner, Rudolf. *How the Spiritual World Projects Into Physical Existence: The Influences of the Dead*. Rudolf Steiner Press, 2014.

ARSON PRESS

https://arsonpress.wixsite.com/arson

Horrific Punctuation
John Reinhart

Where commas scratch poisoned marks, Thor makes an enthusiastic appearance! shotguns make dark holes to mark the end...or maybe the beginning of something new. Zombies, harpies, Odin, Schrödinger's cat, Hermes, yetis, the Loch Ness Monster, and more nightmares are here to remind you that while punctuation can be bad, sometimes it is horrific.

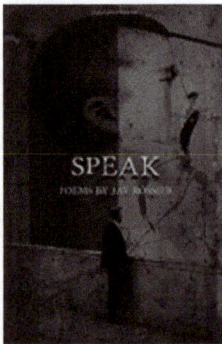

Speak
Jay Rossier

From the author of Living With Chickens, this collection was published shortly after Rossier's death at 51. "I don't know what it is I'm supposed to do. I don't know what the tools are. I don't have the manual." These poems wrestle with the gristle of life: a child hesitant to pick up a kitten, "its loose bag of skin, the bones / and organs sliding around under your fingers." Each one looks life in the eye unafraid to lose the staring contest, but determined to speak.

www.ingramcontent.com/pod-product-compliance
Lightning Source LLC
Chambersburg PA
CBHW070039100426
42740CB00013B/2731